# TEACHING ESL/EFL WITH THE INTERNET
## Catching the Wave

*Authors*

**Carine M. Feyten**

**Michelle D. Macy**

**Jeannie Ducher**

**Makoto Yoshii**

**Eunwook Park**

**Brendan Calandra**

**John Meros**

*Volume Editor*

**Michelle D. Macy**

Merrill
Prentice Hall

Upper Saddle River, New Jersey
Columbus, Ohio

**Vice President and Publisher:** Jeffery W. Johnston
**Managing Editor:** Allyson P. Sharp
**Production Editor:** Kimberly J. Lundy
**Design Coordinator:** Diane C. Lorenzo
**Copyeditor:** Robert L. Marcum
**Cover Designer:** Ali Mohrman
**Cover Image:** Artville/Mick Tarel
**Production Manager:** Pamela D. Bennett
**Director of Marketing:** Kevin Flanagan
**Marketing Manager:** Krista Groshong
**Marketing Services Manager:** Barbara Koontz

This book was set in Times New Roman by Carlisle Communications, Ltd. and was printed and bound by Banta Book Group. The cover was printed by Phoenix Color Corp.

Pearson Education Ltd., *London*
Pearson Education Australia Pty. Limited, *Sydney*
Pearson Education Singapore Pte. Ltd.
Pearson Education North Asia Ltd., *Hong Kong*
Pearson Education Canada, Ltd., *Toronto*
Pearson Educación de Mexico, S.A. de C.V.
Pearson Education—Japan, *Tokyo*
Pearson Education Malaysia Pte. Ltd.
Pearson Education, *Upper Saddle River, New Jersey*

10  9 8 7 6 5 4 3 2 1
ISBN 0-13-088540-1

# PREFACE

## PURPOSE AND RATIONALE OF THIS TEXT

This book is intended as a tool for ESL/EFL instructors who would like to integrate Internet technology into their teaching. A handful of books are currently available that address either how to use computers for language teaching and learning or the principles of language learning with respect to technology. Instructors, however, may feel overwhelmed by the practical aspects of implementing technology in their classes, or by books that present heavy quantities of theory. For these reasons, *Teaching ESL/EFL with the Internet: Catching the Wave is* designed to reconcile both of these important aspects by being **teacher friendly** and **pedagogically sound** with clear and practical features. This book equips instructors with the necessary pedagogical principles for using technology in language classes, while providing them with field-tested sample activities that can be implemented immediately or used as practical guides and frameworks with which to create their own lessons.

*Teaching ESL/EFL with the Internet* integrates the listening, speaking, reading, writing, and cultural skills necessary to achieve communicative competence in the language classroom. Each chapter is organized around a primary skill, and additional skills are woven into each activity. The varied activities capitalize on the authentic and constantly updated nature of the Internet, which enables students to learn in meaningful, relevant, and practical situational contexts. The objectives of each lesson are clearly stated and spotlight higher-order thinking skills. All activities include the appropriate schema-building techniques needed to effectively prepare students to work individually or collaboratively with authentic materials. In addition, each lesson includes suggestions for modifying the activities to other learning levels, as well as ideas for expanding the instruction.

As additional support for the instructor, an entire chapter is devoted to model assessment rubrics, which may be modified and used at the teacher's discretion. A list of instructional tips relevant to the teaching of each key skill is offered in every chapter. Each chapter also contains a simplified list of language-learning strategies designed to focus students' attention on certain aspects of acquisition. Tips on computer use, Internet searches, and identification of potential problems are provided in the Appendix.

This text is not designed for use as a standalone text. Rather, it should help instructors to be more creative and effective in using computers in their classrooms, which in turn will enhance language learning for ESL/EFL students at all levels of proficiency through high school and beyond.

## USING THIS TEXT

### Organization of the Chapters

For ease of use, each chapter of this text has an explicit focus. Although every section emphasizes particular features of language learning, such competencies cannot be taught in isolation from one another. On the contrary, the skills of listening, speaking, reading, writing, and culture are interdependent and should be taught through an integrative approach. As a result, multiple features have been woven into all of the lessons in this book.

### Chapter Guides

The necessity and means of integrating a given language skill into the curriculum explained at the beginning of each chapter in the form of a rationale and guide written by field experts. Each chapter's target skill is woven into the lessons with the goal of promoting highly effective communication in the second/foreign language. Each guide presents, an overall view of the skill, followed by specific teacher tips on its integration, and concludes with a reproducible list of ways for students to incorporate the skill.

### Lesson Use and Adaptability

The lessons in *Teaching ESL/EFL with the Internet* have been carefully designed and field tested. In addition to considering content, site stability, student and instructor interest and enjoyment, implementation time, and difficulty levels, lessons were also composed with multiculturalism and multiple intelligences in mind to appeal to and be effective with a variety of learners. The lessons are ready for immediate implementation and are copy ready. Instructors, however, are encouraged to adapt and modify the lessons according to the characteristics and interests of their student populations, as well as to their own needs and constraints.

### Lesson Time

The timing required for completion of a lesson is indicated on both the title and guide pages of each lesson. Although lessons are based on multiple sessions of 50 minutes, the time necessary to complete each lesson depends on many factors, and instructors may find that adjustments are necessary.

## Activity Assessment

Because the activities in this book are aimed at developing students' proficiencies and widening the scope of the traditional language classroom, they can be considered as meaningful practice for students and do not necessarily demand formal assessment. If, a more formal evaluation of student performance is desirable, however, instructors can choose to use and adapt the rubrics provided in Chapter 6, evaluate the lesson worksheets, or assess the final products of the lessons.

## Technology and Classroom Instruction

Working with computer and Internet technologies requires a certain amount of tolerance for technical problems. While the activities in this book involve a minimum of hardware and software requirements, problems with site stability, connection speed, and so on are to be expected. We highly recommend that instructors check the availability of websites and review the technical aspects of the lesson (i.e., downloads, time requirements, hardware and software requirements, etc.) before students access the Internet. Conducting a dry run of the Internet portion of the activity will prevent most of the problems commonly encountered and will result in increased comfort with and ease of use of the technology for students and instructors alike. Be sure to check the Appendix for further information and tips on working with computers and the Internet.

# PHILOSOPHY OF THIS TEXT

## Instruction of English as a Second/Foreign Language

A second/foreign language can be made more accessible and be better retained when acquisition takes place in a communicative and natural environment enhanced by meaningful and authentic materials that aid in the development of proficiency in all areas of communication and culture. Every effort has been made to employ these features throughout this text.

## Lesson Design and Cognition

All lessons have been carefully designed to provide practitioners with activity models that engage students cognitively, while respecting their levels of proficiency in the target language. The performance objectives provided for each lesson are based on Bloom's Taxonomy (see page viii) and give the instructor useful indications of the type and variety of thinking skills required for successful completion of the tasks. Higher-Order Thinking Skills have been identified with a *HOTS* symbol.

## Lesson Design and Meaning

It is widely believed that a second language is best learned when it is used for meaningful communication rather than rote for drills or memorization. Meaningful task are an important part of each lesson in this book. Accordingly, lessons feature high-interest topics with an emphasis on integrating multiple skills.

## Lesson Design and Authenticity

The use of authentic material has been shown to have a positive effect on students' use and understanding of a second language. Such materials may also be more appealing to learners whose levels of cognitive maturity demand complex and relevant input. The Internet is an ideal source for up-to-date and meaningful authentic information and has therefore been heavily integrated into each lesson.

# ACKNOWLEDGEMENTS

We are very grateful to all who helped and supported us as we designed and wrote this book. Many thanks to Dr. Jeffra Flaitz, Dr. Wei Zhu, and Irene Canton for their guidance and contributions, as well as to the faculty and staff of the English Language Institute of the University of South Florida who endorsed our efforts and helped us to pilot our lesson plans. We would also like to express our thanks to our families and friends who encouraged us during the writing of this book.

# BLOOM'S TAXONOMY

Benjamin Bloom[*] developed a classification of cognitive objectives that is a useful framework for setting lesson goals. The taxonomy includes six levels, ranging from the simple recall to evaluation. The levels are knowledge, comprehension, application, analysis, synthesis, and evaluation. Examples of verbs represented in each level are given here. In this text, lesson objectives are described using such verbs, and those requiring Higher-Order Thinking Skills (those that belong to category four or higher) are marked with a *HOTS* symbol .This textpromotes Higher-Order Thinking Skills in Internet-based activities.

1. **Knowledge or the ability to recall information**

   Arrange, define, duplicate, label, list, memorize, name, order, recognize, relate, recall, repeat, reproduce, state

2. **Comprehension or interpreting information in one's own words**

   Classify, describe, discuss, explain, express, identify, indicate, locate, recognize, report, restate, review, select, translate

3. **Application or using knowledge in a novel situation**

   Apply, choose, demonstrate, dramatize, employ, illustrate, interpret, operate, practice, schedule, sketch, solve, use

   *HOTS* 4. **Analysis or breaking down knowledge into parts and showing interrelationships**

   Analyze, appraise, calculate, categorize, compare, contrast, criticize, differentiate, discriminate, distinguish, examine, experiment, question, test

   *HOTS* 5. **Synthesis or bringing together parts of knowledge to form a whole and solve a problem**

   Arrange, assemble, collect, compose, construct, create, design, develop, formulate, manage, organize, plan, prepare, propose, set up

   *HOTS* 6. **Evaluation or making judgments on the basis of criteria**

   Appraise, argue, assess, attach, choose, compare, defend, estimate, judge, predict, rate, select, support, value, evaluate

---

[*]Bloom, Benjamin. 1956. *Taxonomy of educational objectives: Handbook I: Cognitive domain.* New York: David McKay.

# CONTENTS

NOTE: Every effort has been made to provide accurate and current Internet information in this book. However, the Internet and information posted on it are constantly changing, so it is inevitable that some of the internet addresses listed in this textbook will change.

# HARDWARE REQUIREMENTS

**Ideal:**

- 233+ megahertz processor

- 48+ megabytes RAM

- 16+ megabyte video card *(PC users)*

- 56+ kilobytes/sec. modem

- 32-bit color

- Keyboard

- Mouse

- Color printer

- Sound card (PC users)

- Speakers

- Microphone

**Minimum:**

- 75 megahertz processor

- 32 megabytes RAM

- 8 megabyte video card *(PC users)*

- 28.8 kilobytes/sec. modem

- 256 colors

- Keyboard

- Mouse

- Printer

*For more computer tips, see the Appendix.*

# Good Vibrations:
# Improving Listening Skills

# A Rationale & Guide for Integrating Listening into English Language Instruction

**Michelle Macy & Carine Feyten**

Listening ability is essential to learning any language, particularly since it is the most-used language skill, over speaking, reading, and writing (45% more[*]). There is even considerable evidence that listening may be the *first skill* students should practice and acquire, *preceding* speaking, reading, and writing. Most teachers fully understand the importance of their students being able to listen to and understand the target language, but may not be aware of the many things they can do to optimize the classroom environment and activities to improve students' listening and comprehension abilities. When teachers take an active role in working on their students' listening skills, they are increasing the speed and the quality of language acquisition at all levels of learning. The lessons in this chapter focus on listening, incorporating additional skills into the activities.

In addition to grammar and vocabulary, instructors can actively teach certain behaviors that are meant to help students get the most from a listening activity. These include determining the purpose of the speaker and predicting what the speaker is going to say, as well as identifying key words and phrases that help establish the meaning of the passage based on background knowledge on the topic. Students can learn to focus on overall meaning rather than specific words, and to guess to fill in any gaps. Teachers can help students look for clues beyond the words themselves such as context, body language, and tone of voice.

A practical learning environment can be established as students expand their listening skills and instructors make careful choices of listening material. Teachers must balance what students can comprehend clearly and what would offer a slight challenge at a given level of language study. On one extreme, if the activity is too easy, students may gain little new knowledge and become bored. On the other, overly difficult activities can devolve into mere noise for students, which may lead them to give up. A single authentic text can be the source of many activities at various levels, since it is the activity that determines the difficulty and not, generally, the passage. Beginning students can, for example, be asked to glean rather cursory information from a selection, while advanced students listening to the same piece may be able to understand nearly all of it and carry out a more complex activity. The listening material that students are responsible for at their level of proficiency must be largely understandable, engaging,

---

[*] Rivers, W. (1975). *A practical guide to the teaching of French.* Fairlawn, NJ: Oxford University Press.

and interesting. Degrees of learner familiarity with topic, ability to predict the content, and level of precision of comprehension may increase with students' overall proficiency.

This book includes authentic-language, Internet-based listening activities that range from general identification to comprehension of higher-order ideas, from understanding of details to full understanding and replication of the spoken text.

Listening activities should be approached with an understanding of their importance, as well as a willingness to instruct students in listening strategies and to provide high-quality materials appropriate to their level and age.

---

**To learn more, teachers may wish to consult the following references:**

Brett, P. (1997). A comparative study of the effects of the use of multimedia on listening comprehension. *System,* 25(1): 39–53.

Brindley, G. (1998). Assessing listening abilities. *Annual Review of Applied Linguistics,* 18, 171–191.

Feyten, C. (1991). The power of listening ability: An overlooked dimension in language acquisition. *Modern Language Journal,* 75(2): 173–80.

Feyten, C. (1992). Listening and second language acquisition. *Middle School Journal,* 24(2): 72–75.

Glisan, E. (1988). A plan for teaching listening comprehension: Adaptation of an instructional reading model. *Foreign Language Annals,* 21(1): 9–16.

Herron, C. A. and Seay, I. (1991). The effect of authentic oral texts on student listening comprehension in the foreign language classroom. *Foreign Language Annals,* 24(6): 487–196.

Rivers, W. (1986). Comprehension and production in interactive language teaching. *Modern Language Journal,* 70(1): 1–7.

# TEACHING TIPS FOR LISTENING

### Modeling:

♦ Be a good model for the students and **be patient as you listen** to them when they are attempting to use the target language.

### Preparation:

♦ Evaluate and expand students' **background knowledge** before they listen as it limits the number of possible interpretations.

♦ Have the students do **prelistening** activities to prepare them for the topic, vocabulary and structures, and cultural features they are going to encounter.

♦ Allow students to **predict** meaning from context.

♦ When appropriate, provide visual **cues** to language, such as facial expressions or images. You may lessen these cues as students gain proficiency.

♦ Train students to recognize the sounds of the language.

### Negotiation and Comprehension:

♦ Have students **collaborate** on listening tasks so they can build meaning together.

♦ When appropriate, allow students to hear the passage as many times as needed.

♦ Remember that text length can be short or long, however, short passages may cause students to rely on linear word-by-word comprehension, while longer ones may force them to search for **basic meaning**.

♦ You may even choose to use the same texts with students of different levels, knowing that the type and amount of comprehension will vary between beginning and advanced students.

### Expectations:

♦ Help students understand that they need not know every word. The goals of listening include grasping the **basic meaning** as well as distinguishing sounds and key words.

♦ Keep in mind that different students have different **learning styles**. Auditory learners will progress faster, while others may need more cues to comprehend a passage.

### Motivation:

♦ Topics should be **relevant** to students' interests.

♦ Be certain the listening activity has a **purpose**.

### Level:

♦ Do not fear using **authentic** spoken texts, even with beginning students.

♦ For beginning level, make sure the content is **familiar**.

♦ If the listening activity is too difficult, students' anxiety may rise too high, limiting understanding.

♦ The text does not determine the level, the activity does. Activities may be done at many levels with a single passage.

♦ Not every piece of authentic material is suited to every learner level.

# LISTENING TIPS FOR STUDENTS

♦ Relax and pay attention.

♦ Stay focused on what you are hearing.

♦ Predict what the passage is going to be about.

♦ Try to anticipate what the speaker is going to say.

♦ Try to remember key points in the passage.

♦ Don't try to understand every single word.

♦ Guess meanings when you don't understand.

♦ Ask questions.

♦ Watch for visual cues such as body language and facial expressions.

♦ Listen for verbal cues such as tone of voice.

♦ Learn the culture.

♦ Practice, practice, practice!

# Beach Life
## *Listening for Biographical Information*

| | |
|---|---|
| **Integrated Skills:** | LISTENING; Reading; Speaking |

**Level:** Beginning

**Objectives:**

- Students will extract key biographical information from a written text.

- Students will extract key biographical information from an audio segment.

*HOTS* Students will discriminate between highly similar target language sounds.

**Website Address(es):** http://www.biography.com —*Site for biographies*

   *Visit this site before beginning the lesson to confirm the locations of the necessary links.*

**Suggested Time:** Two 50-minute sessions

**Hardware Requirements:**
- Sound card *(PC users)*
- Headphones or speakers

**Software Requirements:** Real™Audio®

   *To save time, prior to beginning the lesson, download Real™Audio® onto the hard drives of all the computers to be used.*

**Computing Skills:**
- Performing a search
- Downloading

# TEACHER GUIDE

| | |
|---|---|
| **Preactivity Day 1**  | **Schema Building:** <br> 1. Introduce the activity by asking students to name famous movie stars. Ask about American movie stars, then American Western movie stars. If students do not mention John Wayne, provide the name. Show a picture or a movie clip of the actor. <br><br> 2. Review/brainstorm vocabulary for physical characteristics and descriptive adjectives. Have students describe John Wayne. |

| | | |
|---|---|---|
| **Activity Day 1**  | **Grouping:** <br> Individual | **Setup:** <br> Students will read a short biographical segment concerning John Wayne, and complete Part I of the worksheet. They will then listen to an additional audio segment and complete Part II. |

| | |
|---|---|
| | 1. Distribute worksheets, and have students go to the website www.biography.com. On the designated web page, students perform a search *within* the site by typing "John Wayne" (without the quotation marks; capitals optional) into the provided text box and clicking "Find." They then click on the "Wayne, John" link. <br><br> 2. Have students *read* the biographical information and do Part I of the worksheet. <br><br> 3. Have students type "www.biography.com/features/" in the address bar of their browsers. Once on that page, have them scroll down and click on the "BioBytes Archive" link in the BioByte section. <br><br> 4. Have them click on the link for "John Wayne." <br><br> 5. Ask students to listen to the audio file once through, then as many times as necessary in order to complete Part II of their worksheets. |

| | |
|---|---|
| **Postactivity Day 2**  | Have students write a "little known fact" about themselves on a piece of paper (unusual birthplace, special talent, unique hobby, nickname, etc). Collect. <br><br> Make a bingo card with one student fact per square. Have students circulate around the room, asking questions in an attempt to complete a row (horizontal, vertical, or diagonal) or the whole card (see sample on page 10). |

**Tips:** For instructors unfamiliar with Bingo, here is a quick explanation:

Make a numbered list of the facts the students provide in the postactivity (you might even want to add something about yourself). On another sheet of paper, make a bingo card. Have as many boxes as you have facts. Distribute a card to each student, and ask students to randomly place a number in each box (the range of numbers should be equal to the number of facts). Once this is done, distribute the numbered list of facts. Students will attempt to match a person and their fact to a box. Students must go around the room, ask their classmates questions, and get them to sign in the box that corresponds to their fact. The first student to complete a row (or the entire sheet) wins by shouting "Bingo!" (see sample on page 10).

**Student's name:** _____ Date:_____

## WORKSHEET

### PART I. Read the biography and answer the following questions.

1. When was John Wayne born?          _____

2. When did he die?          _____

3. Where did he grow up?          _____

4. What is the name of the movie for which he won an Oscar (Academy Award)?

    _____

5. What movie gave him his "big break" (opportunity)?

    _____

6. What is the name of his final movie?

    _____


### PART II. Listen to the passage and complete the blanks.

1. What are John Wayne's two nicknames?          _____

    _____

2. In what year did he win the Oscar?    _____

3. When he was not acting, he was a national "_____."

4. He commanded "_____."


### Listen and circle the best answer.

1. *Almost two decades after his*
    a) debt          c) date
    b) days          d) death
    *many still regard John Wayne as an American hero.*

2. *At the very*
    a) least          c) listed
    b) list          d) lease
    *he is always remembered as "the Duke."*

3. *He was a man of*
    a) congestion          c) conviction
    b) prediction          d) confection

4. *and a lover of*
    a) light          c) life
    b) night          d) wife

## Activity 1.1

### Further Activities:

1. Show a John Wayne movie or movie clip.

2. Alter or repeat the activity by using a different celebrity with a BioBytes Archive entry (Rosie O' Donnell, Jackie Robinson, Jessica Savitch, etc.).

3. Have students research nicknames of other famous people.

4. Have students present famous movie stars from their own countries.

### Modify the Level:

1. Intermediate students can write their own biographies. As an extension of this, they might then exchange their biographies and introduce/profile a partner.

2. Intermediate students can create a fictitious character and present a biography of that person to the class.

3. Intermediate students can interview native speakers (in person, by email, or by chat room) on their opinions about John Wayne (e.g., his status as a role model or a hero, his acting ability, etc.).

4. Advanced students can create and record (audio or video) a brief speech/biography modeled after the one given on this site.

5. Advanced students can perform a search, find two subjects (politicians, actors, musicians, etc.), and write a paper comparing their lives.

6. Advanced students can interview each other and report to the class. The students should strive to draw out key, informative points to make their presentations lively and interesting.

7. Advanced students can discuss John Wayne as a role model or hero and the changing image of the cowboy in terms of racism, sexism, and the like.

**Sample Bingo Card (use full sheet)**

| 14 | 3 | 1 | 15 | 8 |
|----|----|----|----|----|
| 16 | 11 | 7 | 18 | 12 |
| 5 | 2 | 4 | 20 | 9 |
| 17 | 6 | 19 | 13 | 10 |

**Sample Matching Sheet (use full sheet)**

1. My favorite color is green.
2. I have 5 siblings.
3. I can play the violin.
4. I was born

# On the Wild Side

*Guessing an Animal's Identity*

| | |
|---|---|
| **Integrated Skills:** | LISTENING; Speaking; Reading |
| **Level:** | Beginning |
| **Objectives:** | ■ Students will extract information from a written text on animals. |
| *HOTS* | Students will negotiate for meaning in guessing an animal's identity. |
| *HOTS* | Students will listen to and organize information in order to create a presentation. |
| **Website Address(es):** | http://www.microsoft.com/downloads —*Download Microsoft® NetMeeting® (free)* |
| | http://www.tribal.com —*Download Tribal Voice® Powwow® (free)* |
| | http://www.oaklandzoo.org/atoz/atoz.html —*Animal info* |
| | http://www.seaworld.org/animal_bytes/animal_bytes.html —*Animal info* |
| | http://www.birminghamzoo.com/search/ —*Animal info* |
| **Suggested Time:** | Four 50-minute sessions |
| **Hardware Requirements:** | ■ Sound card *(PC users)* |
| | ■ Headphones or speakers |
| | ■ Microphones |
| **Software Requirements:** | Audio conferencing program (i.e. Microsoft® NetMeeting®, Tribal Voice® Powwow®, Yahoo Messenger, Excite Voice Chat, etc.) |
| | *To save time, prior to beginning of lesson, download audio conferencing program onto the hard drives of all the computers to be used.* |
| | *Practice using the conferencing program so it will be easier to explain to students who are not familiar with it.* |
| **Computing Skills:** | Downloading |
| **Additional Resources:** | ■ *Alternate: Instead of a Web resource on animals, a CD-ROM Encyclopedia is adequate.* |
| | ■ *Alternate: Should an audio conferencing program be inaccessible, students can still be seated back-to-back in pairs for the listening.* |

Activity 1.2       # TEACHER GUIDE

| **Preactivity Day 1**  | **Schema Building:** 1. Introduce the activity by showing students pictures of various animals. Have them think of and list vocabulary words to describe them (i.e., fur, scales, feathers, mammal, reptile, etc.). 2. Continue by discussing animals found locally. **Modeling:** Duplicate and distribute Listener worksheets to the students. To get the whole class online and in listening/speaking mode in your audio conferencing program, play the role of the Speaker, while the students play the role of Listeners. Describe one of the animals you just discussed without saying its name. The students complete the worksheet based on your description, then guess which animal it is. | |
|---|---|---|
| **Activity Days 2–3**  | **Grouping:** Part I: Individuals gathering information on an animal. Part II: Assigned but anonymous pairs in the audio conferencing program. (Assign one student as Listener and one as Speaker). | **Setup:** Students will use the Internet to complete the Speaker worksheet on an animal. In anonymous pairs, students will then describe an animal to a partner using a conferencing program, while keeping their own and the animal's identity a secret. The partner will complete the Listener worksheet based on the Speaker's description. |
| | 1. Give students a Speaker and a Listener worksheet and have them access appropriate websites or an encyclopedia for information on an animal. Ask them to complete the Speaker worksheet. 2. Assign students to the roles of Speakers or Listeners. Next, give each student a login name to use in the conferencing program, as well as the login name of their partner. The login names should not reveal the identities of the students. 3. Students log in to a conferencing program using their assigned pseudonyms and link up with their partners. They access the speaking mode. The Speaker then describes an animal, based on the Speaker worksheet, without revealing the identity of the animal. The Listener records the information on the Listener worksheet. 4. Students switch roles (Listeners become Speakers). | |
| **Postactivity Day 4**  | 1. Have students convert the information they gathered from their partners into a paragraph. 2. Have them then orally present this paragraph to the class, while continuing to hide the identity of their partner's animal. The class attempts to guess the name of the animal based on the description given. (Partners may also be asked to step forward when they recognize the identities of their own animals). | |

**Student's name:** _____ **Date:** _____

## SPEAKER WORKSHEET

**Find information on an animal, so you can explain it to someone else.**

**Animal's Name:**

_____

**Habitat:** Where does it live?

_____

**Physical Characteristics:** What does it look like?

_____

_____

_____

**Eating Habits:** What does it eat?

_____

**Particularities:** Is it endangered? Does it live in only one part of the world? Is it unique in some way?

_____

_____

_____

**Student's name:** _____ **Date:** _____

## LISTENER WORKSHEET

**Answer below as your partner describes an animal to you.**

**Habitat:** Where does it live?

_____

**Physical Characteristics:** What does it look like?

_____

_____

_____

**Eating Habits:** What does it eat?

_____

**Particularities:** Is it endangered? Does it live in only one part of the world? Is it unique in some way?

_____

_____

**Can you guess what animal it is?** _____

**Activity 1.2**

## Further Activities:

1. Have students look for more animals and as a class compose an animal encyclopedia.

2. Narrow the focus to animals of a single area or region.

3. Change the category (trees, plants, flowers, national flags, etc.).

## Modify the Level:

1. Intermediate/advanced students can focus on endangered species and gather detailed information to present to the class.

2. Intermediate/advanced students can research famous *people* and have their classmates try to guess their identities.

# Salty Dog
## *Understanding the Behavior of Dogs*

| | |
|---|---|
| **Integrated Skills:** | LISTENING; Speaking |
| **Level:** | Intermediate |
| **Objectives:** | ▪ Students will recognize and restate a question from an audio file. |
| | ▪ Students will extract key information from an audio file. |
| ₹₹₹₹₹₹<br>*HOTS* | Students will reconstruct the meaning of a listening segment. |
| ₹₹₹₹₹₹<br>*HOTS* | Students will collaborate with peers. |
| | ▪ Students will present their findings orally. |
| **Website Address(es):** | http://www.aaas.org/ehr/sciup/documents/january99.html<br>—*Science questions and answers* |
| **Suggested Time:** | Three 50-minute sessions |
| **Hardware Requirements:** | ▪ Sound card *(PC users)*<br>▪ Headphones or speakers |
| **Software Requirements:** | Real™Audio®<br><br>*To save time, prior to beginning the lesson, download and install Real™Audio® onto the hard drives of all the computers to be used.* |
| **Computing Skills:** | Downloading |
| **Additional Resources:** | *An audiotape of the passages can be requested from the organization should the Internet connection not be available.* |

**Activity 1.3**

# TEACHER GUIDE

| | |
|---|---|
| **Preactivity Day 1**  | **Schema Building:**<br>1.  Ask students about their pets. What strange or funny things do they do? Why do they do these things?<br><br>2.  Ask questions about dogs. Focus on those with probable scientific explanations (e.g., Why do dogs salivate in the presence of food? Why do dogs' tongues hang out?) |

| | | |
|---|---|---|
| **Activity Days 1–2** | **Grouping:**<br>Part I:<br>Individual<br>Part II: Pairs | **Setup:**<br>Students will access a science website where they will listen to questions and answers concerning the behavior of dogs, and complete the worksheet according to the passages. |

1.  Distribute worksheets and have students visit the provided website. In the boxed list, have them click on "Cats and Dogs" (January 14) and then in the main list on "Why is it: Cats and Dogs." Have them listen to the audio file. (They may listen several times). Ask them to complete Part I of the worksheet, which includes identifying the question and recognizing the answers. Once finished, ask students to close their Real™Player® windows.

2.  Group students into pairs, and, in the same website, ask them to scroll down to January 28 and click on "Why is it: Cuts and Dogs." Have them listen and work together to complete Part II of the worksheet, which requires them to listen for detailed information.

| | |
|---|---|
| **Postactivity Day 3**  | 1.  Assign pairs to a variety of "Why is it" topics by date.<br><br>2.  Have two pairs work separately on the same topic, then come together to share and compile their notes.<br><br>3.  Ask them to present their topic to the class. |

Student's name: _____ Date:_____

## WORKSHEET

**PART I. Individual Activity.**

**Listen carefully to the audio file.**

**1. What is the original question?**

_____

_____

**2. Listen again to the audio file, and mark (X) *all* correct answers below.**

_____ Dogs instinctively respond to motion.

_____ Dogs do not like cats.

_____ Dogs are trained to chase cats.

_____ Dogs enjoy chasing cats.

**PART II. Paired Activity.**

**Listen carefully to the audio file.**

**This "Why is it" audio segment is about dogs licking their masters' wounds. You must find out the reasons for this.**

- _____

- _____

- _____

# Activity 1.3

## Further Activities:

1. Have students search this audio archive site for scientific facts about other animals, and present them to the class (they can use presentation software or a poster).

2. Have students search the net for scientific facts and make a presentation (using presentation software or a poster).

## Modify the Level:

1. Beginning students can listen for specific keywords (verbs, adjectives, etc.).

2. Advanced students can create sound files on the "why is it" model. (They can perform net searches on a scientific fact to locate interviews and expert opinions on their topic). Place all student-created sound files into a folder on the hard drive of the computer(s) you are working with, and have students listen to each other's "Why is it" scientific fact. Have them fill out a worksheet and/or write a summary/report.

3. Have advanced students write down questions related to science. After collecting the questions, redistribute them to other students, who then look for the answers on the Internet and present their findings to the class.

# Beach Party
*Identifying Famous People Through Biographies*

| | |
|---|---|
| **Integrated Skills:** | LISTENING; Reading; Speaking |
| **Level:** | Intermediate |

**Objectives:**

*HOTS*   Students will compile biographical information from the Internet.

*HOTS*   Students will reconstruct and record this information as a sound file.

*HOTS*   Students will interpret the sound files and identify the biographical subject.

▪   Students will match the personalities to their descriptions.

**Website Address(es):**   *Click the "Search" button on your browser or use any search engine*

**Suggested Time:**   Three 50-minute sessions

**Hardware Requirements:**
- Sound card *(PC users)*
- Headphones or speakers
- Microphones

     *\*Be aware that some computer operating systems require specialized settings for activating a microphone.*

**Software Requirements:**   Sound recording software

**Computing Skills:**
- Performing a search
- Downloading

# TEACHER GUIDE

| Preactivity Day 1  | **Schema Building:** 1. Introduce the activity by showing students a brief video clip of an event (e.g., a scene from a movie or a news clip), or pictures of people. 2. Ask students to describe the characters in detail (what they were wearing, what they did, what they said, etc). 3. As a class, review/brainstorm words for physical characteristics and descriptive adjectives. | |
|---|---|---|
| **Activity Days 1–2** | **Grouping:** Individual | **Setup:** Students will perform a Web search to look for information on a personality, whose identity they will keep a secret. They will make a recording of themselves presenting this information. They will then listen to all their classmates' sound files, and will try to match each one to the list of personalities on their answer sheet according to the descriptions given by the other students. |
| | 1. Create a "Personalities" folder on the computer(s) in advance so the students will know where to store their sound files. 2. Assign each student to a personality using the list on the answer sheet, page 23 (draw from a hat). 3. Distribute the worksheets and have students perform Web searches on their assigned people. 4. Ask students to record themselves using sound recording software. They are to give information about the individuals they researched, keeping the names a secret. They have a maximum of 60 seconds to do so. 5. Each sound file should be named and saved into the "Personalities" folder. 6 Give students headphones and an answer sheet. 7. Students access and listen to their classmates' sound files and try to match the information with the names on their answer sheet. 8. Collect the answer sheets. | | |
| **Postactivity Day 3** | Have students fully present their assigned personalities to the class. Allow students to choose their preferred mode of presentation (presentation program, poster, show and tell, etc.). | |

**Tips:**

1. It is ***highly recommended*** that you familiarize yourself with the location and use of your sound recording software before you attempt the lesson with your students.

2. You may modify answer sheet provided to accommodate class size, available resources, and target culture.

3. Students can record the information in either the first or third person (e.g., either "I am a 57 year-old male" or "My character is a 57 year-old male").

4. Remind students to randomly name the sound files, so the identities of the personalities remain concealed (e.g., *station2.wav*).

5. Remind students not to read from their worksheet as they record themselves.

6. The "Personalities" folder:
   *Option A:* If using a local area network, be certain that the folder is accessible to all computers.
   *Option B:* If not locally networked, place the folder on the desktop of the computers, and have students circulate from one computer to the next.
   *Option C:* If using a single computer, place all the sound files into a single folder and place the folder on the desktop of the computer.

7. Should the sound recording software be unavailable, students can record themselves on audiocassettes.

**Activity 1.4**

Student's name: _____Date:_____

## WORKSHEET

**Find the following information.**

**Name of the personality:** _____

**Nationality:** _____

**Male or Female:** _____

**Date of birth:** _____

**Date of death:** _____
(if applicable)

**Marital status:** _____
(if applicable)

**Physical description:** _____

_____

_____

**Other characteristics:** _____
(if applicable)

_____

**Profession:** _____

**Accomplishments:** _____
*(Why is this person famous?)*

_____

_____

Student's name: _____Date:_____

## ANSWER SHEET

Write the sound file name in front of the personality name.

| | | | |
|---|---|---|---|
| _____ | Albert Einstein | _____ | Pablo Neruda |
| _____ | Marie Curie | _____ | Billie Jean King |
| _____ | Elvis Presley | _____ | Nadia Comaneci |
| _____ | John Lennon | _____ | Charles Lindbergh |
| _____ | Pablo Picasso | _____ | Jacques-Yves Cousteau |
| _____ | Claude Monet | _____ | Marlene Dietrich |
| _____ | King Kamehameha | _____ | Elizabeth Taylor |
| _____ | King Hussein of Jordan | _____ | Jackie Chan |
| _____ | Margaret Thatcher | _____ | Wolfgang Amadeus Mozart |
| _____ | Indira Gandhi | _____ | Ludwig van Beethoven |
| _____ | Nelson Mandela | _____ | Marie Antoinette |
| _____ | Martin Luther King, Jr. | _____ | Benjamin Franklin |
| _____ | Bartolome de Las Casas | _____ | George Washington |
| _____ | Ernest Hemingway | _____ | Akio Morita |
| _____ | Gabriel Garcia Marquez | _____ | Rachel Carson |
| _____ | Mark Twain | _____ | Valentina Vladinirovna Tereshkova |

**Activity 1.4**

## Further Activities:

1. Modify the postactivity by having students dress up (simple costumes) as their assigned personalities and present themselves informally in the context of a party. As a group they should circulate around the room and practice chatting in the guise of their characters.

2. Have students design a survey, and interview native speakers (in person, by key pal, or in a chatroom) about their knowledge of the personalities in the activity. (e.g., Do you know when Einstein lived? Why is Charles Lindbergh famous?)

## Modify the Level:

1. Beginning students can limit the activity to describing themselves and guessing each other's identities.

2. The activity can be modified for advanced students to have them research a historical event and orally record a description of it. As in the original activity, the actual name of the event should remain a secret. Instead of using an answer sheet, the students should listen to the description, make notes, and work together in small groups to identify the event.

# The Island Daily
## *Using the News to Learn*

| | |
|---|---|
| **Integrated Skills:** | LISTENING; Reading, Speaking, Writing |
| **Level:** | Advanced |
| **Objectives:** | ▪ Students will predict key points in an authentic news report. |
| | ▪ Students will extract the main ideas from the content. |
| | ▪ Students will discuss and revise their interpretations of the content. |
| *HOTS* | Students will analyze the content of the news and extract information. |
| *HOTS* | Students will summarize and discuss the information they gathered. |
| **Website Address(es):** | http://foxnews.com/video —*News site* |
| | *Be certain that the correct boxes for modem speed and type of media player are checked.* |
| **Suggested Time:** | Two 50-minute sessions |
| **Hardware Requirements:** | ▪ Sound card *(PC users)* |
| | ▪ Headphones or speakers |
| **Software Requirements:** | Real™Video™ |
| | *To save time, prior to beginning the lesson, download and install Real™Video™ from www.real.com/products/player/index.html onto the hard drives of all the computers to be used.* |
| **Computing Skills:** | Downloading |

**Activity 1.5**

# TEACHER GUIDE

| | |
|---|---|
| **Preactivity**<br>**Day 1**<br> | **Schema Building:**<br><br>1. Lead a class discussion on current news events. What's happening today? Ask students if they saw the news yesterday. If so, what was the main news story?<br><br>2. Share any information the students might find interesting about the news. |
| **Activity**<br>**Day 1**<br> | **Grouping:** / **Setup:** (see below) |

**Grouping:**
Part I : Individual
Parts II and III:
Pairs

**Setup:**
Students will predict, analyze, and discuss information from an Internet-based news video clip.

1. Distribute worksheets and have students watch a news video clip from the site listed above (or any site with news video) and ask them to complete Part I. After 10 minutes, have students turn their worksheets over so they cannot see their answers.

2. Pair students and ask them to discuss the information they found. Suggest they make notes on any new information they gather from their partners. After 10 more minutes, have students look again at their worksheets and collaborate to complete Part II.

3. Allow students to return to the video clip, watch it again and read the accompanying text. They then complete Part III of the worksheet.

4. Have students share with the class what they gathered, as well as their own personal opinions concerning the topic.

| | |
|---|---|
| **Postactivity**<br>**Day 2**<br> | Assign as homework for students to watch or listen to the news (TV or radio) to see if there are any further developments on the story covered in class. They are to summarize the content of the news story in 2–3 paragraphs and e-mail their work to you before the next class. |

 **Tips:**   1. Examine the content of the video clips before class.

2. Be aware that not all news stories have accompanying video.

**Student's name:** _____ **Date:** _____

## WORKSHEET

**PART I.**    **Follow the instructions below and complete the blanks.**

1. Choose a news headline and write it in the space provided.

_____

2. Before clicking on the "Play" button for the headline, what do you think the clip will be about? Write three words or phrases that express your prediction.

   A. _____    B. _____    C. _____

**Click on the "Play" button for the headline and watch the entire clip one time without stopping. If necessary, watch the whole clip again without stopping.**

## WAIT FOR INSTRUCTIONS

**PART II.**    **With your partner, look again at the predictions you wrote for Part I, number 2. Have they changed? If so, indicate the changes here.**

A. _____    B. _____    C. _____

**PART III.**    **Click "Play" on the news headline again and watch the clip again. This time try to briefly answer the following questions.**

1.  What happened?    _____

_____

_____

2.  Who was involved?    _____

_____

3.  Where did it happen?    _____

_____

4.  When did it happen?    _____

5.  How did it happen?    _____

_____

_____

6. Why did it happen?    _____

_____

_____

**If you still have time, read any of the *related* news stories on the website. You may find additional information about your story.**

## Activity 1.5

**Further Activities:**

1. Assign students to websites associated with different news organizations, such as CNN, NBC, BBC, etc. In small groups, students can share the similarities and differences in the ways different organizations report the news.

2. Have students role play reporting the news as anchor people.

3. Have students prepare a formal essay expressing their opinions on the issue.

**Modify the Level:**

1. Beginning students can limit the exercise to just predicting the content of the video based on what they see and are able to understand.

2. Ask beginning students to identify the words they recognize from the audio.

3. Intermediate students can complete the worksheet through question 4 of Part III.

4. Intermediate students can complete the entire worksheet if more background information is supplied to prepare them in the preactivity.

# The Waves of Our Lives
## *Interpreting Soap Opera Subplots*

| | |
|---|---|
| **Integrated Skills:** | LISTENING; Reading, Speaking |
| **Level:** | Advanced |
| **Objectives:** | |

- Students will identify and summarize soap opera subplots.

*HOTS* Students will collaborate to prepare for listening.

*HOTS* Students will interpret and record events.

*HOTS* Students will compare their appraisals of recorded events.

- Students will predict future events.

**Website Address(es):**

http://www.tvguide.com/soaps/ —*American soap opera update*
➔Click on the "Daily Updates" link➔Look for the "Select a Soap" menu➔Click on the down arrow➔Click on a soap opera

http://www.spe.sony.com/soapcity —*American soap opera update*
➔Look for "Soap Updates"➔Look for "The Weekly Buzz On . . . "
➔Click on a soap opera

http://members.aol.com/soaplinks/index.html#Non-US —*British soap opera links*

Click the "Search" button on your browser or use any search engine for soaps in other anglophone countries

**Suggested Time:** Three to four 50-minute sessions

**Software Requirements:** *Verify before class that the browsers on your computers (e.g., Netscape®, Microsoft® Internet Explorer) support the site. If not, download the necessary plug-ins in advance.*

**Additional Resources:** **VCR**

*You will need to prerecord two brief video clips from the soap opera of your choice to complete the preactivity.*

*You will also need to record one full episode of a soap opera to complete the activity.*

# TEACHER GUIDE

| | |
|---|---|
| **Preactivity Day 1**  | **Schema Building:** |
| | 1. Introduce the concept of a soap opera by showing a brief, prerecorded video clip (VCR) from any typical episode. Discuss the soap opera as a genre, as well as what kinds of soap operas play in the students' home countries. |
| | 2. Discuss the popularity of the soap opera, and the resulting fan magazines, clubs, and websites devoted to reviewing and predicting the story lines. |
| | 3. Mention the concept of subplots, or the idea of threads of a story being woven together. |
| | **Modeling:** |
| | Show another prerecorded video clip (VCR) from a soap opera (a full scene). Explain to students that the scene revolves around an *event*, a *character* or *characters*, and a *promise* or a *problem*. After the clip, discuss and define each of those elements for that scene. Point out to the students how much they extracted from the scene because they were *prepared* to listen. |

| | | |
|---|---|---|
| **Activity Days 2–3**  | **Grouping:** Small groups | **Setup:** In preparation for viewing a full episode together, students will access an Internet-based soap opera update site to extract the central themes. |
| | 1. After you have decided on a soap opera (from which you will record today's episode) distribute worksheets and have students access the "Daily Update" on the provided website. First, have students read about and make a list or chart of the characters. Then, ask them to take notes on the various subplots within the soap opera, and discuss and complete the Preactivity worksheet. | |
| | 2. In the next session, show the class the entire episode of the soap you recorded yesterday. Have them complete their Activity worksheet. | |

| | |
|---|---|
| **Postactivity Day 4** | Ask students to watch the following episode (at home or in class), or access the website again several days later and read the latest update. Discuss whether their predictions came true. |

 **Tips:**

1. Recommended timeline:
   **Day 1:** Students access the Internet site on the events of the soap opera from the *previous* day. Meanwhile, record today's episode.
   **Day 2:** Show recorded episode from Day 1.

2. To help students understand the episode more clearly, replay each scene once or twice before continuing to give students an opportunity to reflect. (This will probably stretch the time limit on the activity, however).

3. Be cautious of explicit scenes. Some students may be particularly sensitive.

4. Note: This lesson is best suited to ESL settings.

**Students' names:** _____**Date:**_____

| PREACTIVITY WORKSHEET | ACTIVITY WORKSHEET |
|---|---|
| 1. What is the title of the soap opera? _____ | **View the episode and answer below.** |
| | How did each of the subplots evolve? Are there any new twists or characters? |
| 2. What are the current subplots of the soap opera? | _____ |
| A (event, character(s), promise/problem): _____ _____ _____ _____ _____ | _____ _____ _____ _____ _____ _____ _____ |
| B (event, character(s), promise/problem): _____ _____ _____ _____ _____ | _____ _____ _____ _____ _____ _____ |
| C (event, character(s), promise/problem): _____ _____ _____ _____ _____ | Predict what will happen tomorrow: _____ _____ _____ _____ |
| Additional subplots: _____ _____ _____ _____ | _____ _____ _____ _____ |

**Activity 1.6**

## Further Activities:

1. Have students create and act out the following episode of the soap opera.

2. Have students write a soap opera for the class using one another as the characters.

3. Ask students to find out more about a specific character or actor.

4. Alternate: Have students go to the website http://gopbi.com/community/groups/ghfanclub/Audio_Recaps_of_the_.html and listen to audio versions of the soap opera updates.

## Modify the Level:

Intermediate students can access and read the Internet site. Have them make a list of characters. Students can then view an episode and attempt to identify the characters according to the Internet-based descriptions of their actions and interactions.

# Verbal Ventures: Fostering Oral Proficiency

# A Rationale & Guide for Integrating Speaking into English Language Instruction

## Michelle Macy

Speaking a second language is an important skill to practice and to acquire, but it is a long and difficult road to native-like expertise for most students. This is because speaking involves many complex abilities, among them listening, comprehension, clarification, and ultimately, production. In addition to these cognitive skills, students must also learn to match their body language, tone, vocabulary, formality level, and so forth to the situation in which they are speaking. Due to this complexity, the act of speaking in a second language is often one fraught with apprehension and consternation for students. It is therefore a skill requiring a great deal of practice to improve one's abilities and to overcome anxiety. When teachers can offer students both numerous opportunities to speak and a variety of speaking situations, students can make confident and steady progress. The lessons in this chapter concentrate on speaking, while incorporating additional skills in the activities.

Teachers can do many things to help their students along the road to oral proficiency in a second language. They should be certain that activities, as well as their own use of the target language, are not going beyond students' listening and comprehension abilities, or learners may not be able to reply adequately in a given situation. Students can be taught to hear and produce the sounds of the target language and can be made aware of the importance of sentence intonation and word stress. Teachers can aid students in speaking by teaching them ways to be more easily understood. Strategies such as hesitating, gesturing and paraphrasing can be invaluable when learners encounter difficulties while talking. Initially, emphasis should be placed on students' communication of ideas, rather than on error correction. Later, as students' abilities increase, greater emphasis can be placed on accuracy.

Teachers should augment these approaches with carefully chosen activities. The speaking activities should be purposeful, with an emphasis on negotiation of meaning and on giving students ample opportunities to practice their speaking skills. The environment should be comfortable and nonthreatening, to encourage risk-taking behaviors and therefore extended practice with the target language. Success can lead to confidence, which can in turn lead learners to attempt tasks of increasing complexity and requiring progressively greater competence.

A successful speaking environment demands a variety of speaking activities ranging from simple oral tasks to extensive discussions giving students the chance to gradually improve their speaking abilities and approach fluency.

---

**To learn more, teachers may wish to consult the following references:**

Galloway, V., and Herron, C. (eds.). (1995). *Research within reach II*. Valdosta, Ga: SCOLT.

Hoff-Ginsberg, E. (1997). *Language development*. Pacific Grove, CA: Brooks/Cole.

# TEACHING TIPS FOR SPEAKING

**Modeling:**
- Adhere to the target language.
- Adapt your speech in speed and complexity to the level of the students.

**Preparation:**
- Teach students compensation skills to make up for lacks in vocabulary or grammar (such as talking around the meaning of something when the actual word isn't coming to mind).
- Give students preparation in vocabulary and grammar.
- Teach students pronunciation, intonation, and word stress skills.

**Negotiation:**
- Teach students to use supplementary forms of expression, such as body language, gestures, etc.
- Have students practice speaking with one another in activities that require an exchange of purposeful information.
- Do not be afraid that students will reinforce incorrect forms by practicing together. The benefits of students working together far outweigh any potential disadvantages such as error transfer.

**Expectations:**
- Be aware that forcing students to speak before they are ready may be detrimental to their progress.

- Be **patient** and allow students adequate time to express themselves.
- Keep in mind that accuracy will increase with time and with practice.
- Be aware that students may not be able to remember a structure immediately after you have taught it. Review and give them ample practice.
- Don't forget that students may understand a form in their minds, but may not be able to produce it right away.

**Motivation:**
- Choose activities **relevant** to students' interests.
- Be certain the speaking activity has a communicative **purpose**.
- Remember that the main goal of speaking is maintaining the flow of **communication**, rather than perfect accuracy.

**Level:**
- Pair students with different levels of proficiency.
- Encourage students to balance accuracy and fluency.
- Do not expect beginning students to be perfectly accurate or error free.

# SPEAKING TIPS FOR STUDENTS

♦ Relax and speak naturally.

♦ Learn to compensate for difficult words or grammatical structures by substituting others.

♦ Remember that if someone doesn't understand you, it's not a disaster—just rephrase it.

♦ Be aware of speaking etiquette in the culture whose language you are learning.

♦ Listen carefully in conversations.

♦ Try to anticipate what the other speaker is going to say.

♦ Ask questions when you don't understand.

♦ Your speech does not have to be perfect to be understood.

♦ Use visual cues, such as body language and facial expressions.

♦ Use verbal cues, such as tone of voice.

♦ It's okay to make mistakes.

♦ Take your time, and speak when you are ready.

♦ Look for opportunities to practice.

♦ Practice, practice, practice!

# Tropical Storm
## *Planning Around the Weather Forecast*

| | | |
|---|---|---|
| **Integrated Skills:** | | SPEAKING; Reading; Listening |

| | | |
|---|---|---|
| **Level:** | | Beginning |

**Objectives:**

*HOTS*    Students will collaborate to plan activities.

*HOTS*    Students will locate and interpret weather forecasts on the Web.

*HOTS*    Students will select activities corresponding to the weather forecast.

*HOTS*    Students will discuss their respective choices.

**Web site address(es):**

http://citylink.neosoft.com/citylink/ —*City information*
➔Click on a state➔click on a city name

http://www.lonelyplanet.com/dest/ —*City information*
➔Click on a continent➔Click on a country➔Click on a city➔(Click on "Attractions" if necessary)

> *For larger cities, use "www.weather.com"*
> ➔Look for "Weather Information"➔ click on "World Weather"➔(Once the page is loaded, page down and select a region/country, then a city name)
>
> *For smaller cities, click the "Search" button on your browser or use any search engine.*

**Suggested Time:**    Two 50-minute sessions

**Computing Skills:**    Performing a search

# TEACHER GUIDE

| | |
|---|---|
| **Preactivity Day 1**  | **Schema Building:** <br> 1. Introduce the activity by telling students about a favorite vacation you took, and then by asking them to recall one of their own. <br><br> 2. The class generates a list of words related to vacations and weather, such as *reservations (nouns), cancel, visit (verbs), near, far, warm, rainy,* etc. <br><br> 3. Encourage students to make connections between certain activities and the weather (e.g., A windy day is good for flying a kite). |

| | | |
|---|---|---|
| **Activity Day 1**  | **Grouping:** Small groups | **Setup:** Students will use websites to find vacation destinations (a city to visit), and information about things to do there. They will then access the five-day weather forecast for the city, and plan activities consistent with the predicted weather. |

| | |
|---|---|
| | 1. Give each group a worksheet and have students access appropriate websites, completing Part I as they proceed. <br><br> 2. Students discuss and agree on a city to visit for a three-day vacation, as well as on the activities they would like to do there. <br><br> 3. Groups locate and interpret the three-day weather forecast for that city and complete Part II of the worksheet accordingly. (Activities chosen should match the predicted weather). |

| | |
|---|---|
| **Postactivity Day 2**  | Have students stand and move about the room as if they were at a party. Students greet one another and discuss their vacation plans. |

 **Tips:**

1. If necessary, provide students with additional guidance in locating the relevant information. Helpful keywords may include the city name and "entertainment" or "guide."

2. The weather forecast often gives little information. For some, it will be enough. Those who can handle more might want to compare the weather report on a number of forecast sites.

3. Review how to form questions before the lesson.

4. During the postactivity, be certain that students are circulating, using realistic greetings, and speaking to students outside of their own group.

**Activity 2.1**

Students' names: _____ Date:_____

## WORSHEET

─────────────────────────────────────────────────────────

### PART I.

1. **Talk about which city your group would like to go to on a three-day vacation. Where does your group want to go?**

   _____

2. **List three activities your group will do in the city.**

   *Activity 1:* _____    *Website:*  http://_____

   *Activity 2:* _____    *Website:*  http://_____

   *Activity 3:* _____    *Website:*  http://_____

3. **Check the weather forecast for the city your group will visit. How will the weather be for the next three days?**

   *Day 1:*                    *Day 2:*                    *Day 3:*

─────────────────────────────────────────────────────────

### PART II.

**Which activities will you do?  Write the answers. Think about the weather as you write.**

| *Example* | *We will* surf. | *. . . because the weather will be*   sunny and nice. |
|---|---|---|
| **Day 1:** | **We will** | **. . . because the weather will be** |
| **Day 2:** | **We will** | **. . . because the weather will be** |
| **Day 3:** | **We will** | **. . . because the weather will be** |

# Activity 2.1

## Further Activities:

1. Students may present their group's travel plans to the whole class.

2. Students may report on the travel plans of another student.

3. Students will look up the forecast for their home cities and then do a weather report (reporting done in small groups).

## Modify the Level:

1. Intermediate students can plan a detailed itinerary of a trip, taking the weather into account. They can discuss in groups what clothing and equipment is necessary to accomplish their adventure. Have them look for places online where they might buy clothing and equipment appropriate to their activities and the weather.

2. Intermediate/advanced students can interview one another about the climate and the tourist attractions in their home cities.

3. Advanced students might recount stories about the weather and past vacations that they have taken. For example: "My family and I planned to go to Managua to see my grandparents. We had only been in the city for two days when a hurricane came and everyone had to leave. My whole family, including my grandparents, went back to my house and we stayed there until it was safe."

4. Advanced students can hold a discussion on weather and natural disasters. What's typical of their home countries? Do they have tornadoes? Earthquakes? Wildfires? Volcanoes? Have any of the students ever encountered such phenomena firsthand? Groups may be assigned a particular item and asked to research online and prepare a class report on where and why such events occur.

# Cruising
## *Selecting a Car*

| | |
|---|---|
| **Integrated Skills:** | SPEAKING; Listening; Culture |
| **Level:** | Beginning |

**Objectives:**

- Students will discuss their preferences for vehicles.

- Students will define and focus their search.

*HOTS* Students will negotiate the selection of a car.

*HOTS* Students will collect and organize information.

**Website Address(es):**    http://www.automallusa.net/indexcar.html —*Cars for sale*

**Time:**    Two 50-minute sessions

# TEACHER GUIDE

| | |
|---|---|
| **Preactivity Day 1**  | **Schema Building:** <br> 1. Ask students about the importance and use of cars in their own cultures. How easy is it to get a driver's license? At what age can they legally drive? <br><br> 2. Lead a class discussion on the importance of cars in American culture. Use pictures, supporting text, TV commercials, and/or movie scenes. <br><br> 3. Have students brainstorm the car vocabulary they know, and make a list (supplementing where necessary). <br><br> 4. Have students brainstorm the many ways to buy a car. |
| **Activity Day 2**  | **Grouping:** Pairs     **Setup:** Students will negotiate and agree on a car to purchase together. They will consider use, size, kind, color, and features. <br><br> 1. Give each student pair a copy of the worksheet. Each pair discusses and agrees on a set of criteria for the purchase of a car, completing Part I as they proceed. <br><br> 2. Students then go to the car dealer site indicated, and complete Part II of the worksheet. They are to select four cars that meet the criteria established in Part I. <br><br> 3. Once they have made their selections, students must compare the four cars in terms of aesthetics, options, and so on, and agree on the car they want to buy. |
| **Postactivity Day 2**  | Have students leave their dream car on the screen once they have located it. One member from each pair circulates around the room (so half of the class is moving around) and visit all of the other "booths." Meanwhile, the remaining student stays at the computer acting as a salesperson, providing information and answering questions about their car. Students switch roles after 15 minutes. Finally, the class holds a secret ballot to vote for the best car of all. Tally the votes on the board. |

 **Tips:**   1. Review question words, question formation, and color words.

         2. Use visual support in the preactivity to clarify the vocabulary. It might also be useful to provide a sheet explaining automobile features.

         3. Consider rewarding the winners of the postactivity vote.

Students' names: _____ Date:_____

## WORKSHEET

**PART I.   You and your friend want to buy a new car together. Discuss the vehicle you want, and come to an agreement.**

**Answer the following questions together:**

1.   What will we use the vehicle for? (recreation, going to work, going to school, etc.)

   _____

2.   What size vehicle do we want (subcompact, compact, fullsize, luxury)?

   _____

3.   What type of vehicle do we want (sedan, coupe, convertible, SUV, van, truck, 4X4)?

   _____

4.   What color do we like?

   _____

5.   What features do we want (comfort, speed, safety features, options, automatic transmission, etc.)?

   _____

**PART II.   Choose four cars. They must match your answers in Part I.**

*Example: Name of car:*    *Cadillac, Seville*
        *Likes:*    *Comfortable, looks nice, prestigious*
        *Dislikes:*    *Too big, uses too much gasoline, too expensive*

**Name of car:** _____
**Likes:** _____
**Dislikes:** _____

**Name of car:** _____
**Likes:** _____
**Dislikes:** _____

**Name of car:** _____
**Likes:** _____
**Dislikes:** _____

**Name of car:** _____
**Likes:** _____
**Dislikes:** _____

**Look again at the four vehicles.  Choose your favorite.**

   Which car did you choose? _____

   Why? _____

# Activity 2.2

## Further Activities:

1. *Alternative:* Have students exchange worksheets with another pair of students after completing only Part I. The other pair then attempts to find vehicles that match the first pair's requirements.

2. *Alternative*: Give students a defined budget to limit the range of vehicles they may choose from.

3. If any students in the class own cars, have them explain to the others what their car looks like and why they bought it. Have students look for a picture of their car on the Internet to show to the class.

## Modify the Level:

1. Intermediate students may use the same Internet site; however have students role play a client–dealer interaction (use bargaining skills) in the postactivity.

2. Intermediate students may work in pairs as drivers and mechanics. Students must explain what is wrong with their cars and the mechanics must estimate the time and the cost for repairs.

3. Intermediate students may work in pairs as driving instructors and students. Review imperatives (commands) before beginning.

4. Advanced students can replace cars with other items, such as bikes, computers, outdoor equipment, and so on.

# Get a Job!
## *Preparing a Résumé & Job Interview*

| | |
|---|---|
| **Integrated Skills:** | SPEAKING; Writing; Listening; Reading |
| **Level:** | Intermediate |

**Objectives:**

- Students will extract relevant information from the Web on job descriptions and requirements.

 Students will compose a resume.

- Students will practice expressing themselves in job interviews.

- Students will use contextually appropriate manners, gestures, voice register.

 **Website Address(es):**

http://www.internetsourcebook.com/jobs/ —*Company search*
➔Look for "Company Profiles"➔Click on "All Industries"➔Look for "Browse by Name"➔click on the first letter in a company's name

http://myjobsearch.com/company.html —*Job site*
➔Click on a company name

http://www.intel.com/jobs/index.htm —*Job site for Intel Corp.*
➔Click on "Current Jobs"➔Click a country➔Complete form & submit

http://jobsmart.org/tools/resume/samples.htm —*Résumé site*

 **Suggested Time:** Five 50-minute sessions

 **Software Requirements:** Word processing program

 **Computing Skills:**

- Performing a search
- Working with a template in a word processing program

# TEACHER GUIDE

| | |
|---|---|
| **Preactivity Day 1**  | **Schema Building:**<br>1. Ask students what kinds of jobs they have had or would like to have.<br>What kinds of jobs do people in their families have?<br>When they look for a job in their home countries, how do they go about it?<br>What are the most important aspects of a job to them (e.g., salary, vacation time, intellectual stimulation, etc.)?<br>2. Discuss the procedures of an interview.<br>Talk about what kinds of body language, speech, dress, and etiquette are appropriate during an interview. Discuss what types of questions an interviewer is likely to ask.<br>3. Explain what a résumé is and show students a copy of one. Discuss the elements a résumé should contain. |

| | | |
|---|---|---|
| **Activity Days 2–4**  | **Grouping:**<br>Pairs and individuals | **Setup:**<br>Students will prepare for role play as both interviewers and job applicants. |

<table>
<tr><td></td><td>
1. Pair students and have them discuss the types of jobs they would eventually like to have, as well as the types of companies that interest them.<br><br>
2. Have individual students write a résumé using a template from a word processing program. (Many résumé samples are also available on the Internet to use as models).<br><br>
3. Individuals search the Internet for a company that meets the needs and wishes expressed by their partners, and gather detailed information about that company.<br><br>
4. Students return to their pairs in either the interviewer or job applicant roles.<br><br>
5. Distribute the worksheets and review vocabulary. Applicants pretend to arrive for a job interview. They meet the company representative (interviewer), submit their résumé, and undergo the interview. Applicants and interviewers complete the section of the worksheet appropriate to their role.<br><br>
6. Applicants and interviewers switch roles and complete the worksheet.
</td></tr>
</table>

| | |
|---|---|
| **Postactivity Day 5** | **Class Discussion:**<br>1. Which companies did applicants like the best?<br><br>2. What applicant qualities did the interviewers prefer? |

 **Tips:**

1. If time is a concern, complete the résumé as an out-of-class activity.

2. To ensure that students gather enough company information before the interview, offer them parameters based on the worksheet.

3. Request that students come to the "job fair" as if it were real (i.e., dress nicely, have résumés printed on résumé paper, etc.)

4. Model interview behavior for students, emphasizing speaking naturally, which requires making eye contact throughout the majority of the interview and not reading from the worksheet verbatim.

5. Résumé templates can be found with most word processing programs. For example, in Microsoft® *Word*, users can find such templates by clicking on File in the menu bar, then New, then Other Documents. Check your word processing program in advance.

6. To save time, assign all or part of the postactivity a written homework.

**Student's name:** _____Date:_____

# INTERVIEW WORKSHEET

TO BE COMPLETED BY THE APPLICANT:

Name of the company: _____

What does the company do?: _____

Location(s) of company headquarters and other offices:

_____

Number of Employees: _____

Company's Assets/Revenue/Net Income: _____

Employee Benefits (health insurance, etc.): _____

Starting Salaries: _____

Characteristics and Strengths of the company: _____

_____

_____

TO BE COMPLETED BY THE INTERVIEWER:

Applicant's Name: _____

Country of Origin: _____

Languages Spoken: _____

Educational Background:

_____

_____

Experience: _____

_____

_____

Description of applicant's strengths (what he or she can do well/special skills):

_____

_____

**Activity 2.3**

## Further Activities:

1. Have students either compose a thank-you letter to the company interviewer, or to the applicant for applying.

2. Have students go outside of the classroom to interview people on what they do for a living, how they got their jobs, and so on.

3. Have students post their résumés on the Internet.

## Modify the Level:

1. Advanced students may consult the Internet for common interview questions and tips before the actual interviews.

2. Advanced students can make reports on the founders of various large companies, discussing how they got their start and what made them successful.

3. Advanced students can compile a list of strategies useful for job searches and interviews.

# Surfing Safari
### *Planning a Trip to a National Park*

| | |
|---|---|
| **Integrated Skills:** | SPEAKING; Listening; Reading; Culture |
| **Level:** | Intermediate |

**Objectives:**

*HOTS* — Students will work together to read authentic information and analyze the content.

■ Students will discuss and plan a trip to a national park.

*HOTS* — Students will present and critique oral presentations.

**Website Address(es):**

http://www.gorp.com/gorp/resource/US_National_Park/
parkmap.htm —*U.S. map with national park locations &
additional park information*

http://www.nps.gov/yose/  —*General information*

http://www.yosemitepark.com  —*Park overview*

http://www.nps.gov/yose/yo_visit.htm  —*Site and area*

http://www.nps.gov/yose/event.htm  —*Events at the park*

http://www.nps.gov/yose/camping.htm
—*Camping informaiton*

http://www.nps.gov/yose/ctab1.htm  —*Camping guide and
rates*

**Suggested Time:** Two 50-minute sessions

**Additional Resources:** U.S. map, including national and state parks

| | |
|---|---|
| **Preactivity Day 1**  | **Schema Building:** <br> 1. Ask students if they have any parklands protected by the government in their countries. <br><br> 2. Show students a map and point out the locations of several national and state parks. <br><br> 3. Share photos, slides, video, magazine pictures, and so on of a national or state park. <br><br> 4. Next, ask the students to locate Yosemite National Park (or any park with a detailed website) on the map. Have they heard of this park before? |

| | **Grouping:** <br> Groups | **Setup:** <br> Students will plan a trip to a national or state park. |
|---|---|---|
| **Activity Day 2**  | | 1. Give each group a worksheet and tell them to access the websites provided (or alternate park sites, if desired). <br><br> 2. While visiting a website, students complete Part I of the worksheet, which asks basic questions about the park. <br><br> 3. Next, students proceed to Part II, where they discuss and plan a trip to the park and reply to the questions listed. Each group must come to an agreement on what they will do together. |

| | |
|---|---|
| **Postactivity Day 2**  | Have the groups present their plans to the class with explanations of why they chose what they did, while the remaining students ask questions. Each member should be responsible for a portion of the presentation. <br> Ask students to evaluate their own and others' presentations (rubric). |

 **Tips:**

1. You may assign different groups to different parks for more interesting comparisons in the postactivity.

2. You may wish to alter the questions on the worksheet according to specific websites.

3. A U.S. map Internet site is provided, but a large pull-down map may be easier to read.

4. Students may look for state park information, but national park websites are usually quite detailed.

5. Remind students to budget their time as they search and plan.

Students' names: _____ Date:_____

## WORKSHEET

**PART I.   Answer the following questions.**

Where is _____ **Park located?** _____
          (name of park)

**During what hours can you find the park open?** _____

**Is the park closed on certain days (i.e., national holidays)?**
**Which ones?**                                    _____

**If you come in your car, how much do you have to pay for entry?** _____

**To visit the entire park, how long do you need to stay?** At least  ( _____ ) days

**PART II.    You and your friends will visit a park on a field trip next month. You will have three days to stay at the park and you must decide which activities your group will do during your stay. Please establish your team's three-day plan, including**

**What kind of activities would you like to participate in and why?**

_____

_____

_____

**Where in the park will you go to do these activities?**

_____

_____

_____

**What kind of transportation will you use (1) to reach the park, and (2) in the park? Why?**

_____

_____

_____

**Where do you want to stay for the night and why? (lodging)**

_____

_____

## Activity 2.4

### Further Activities:

1. *Alternate*: Have students focus on only one aspect of the park.

2. Have different groups focus on different parks.

3. Ask students to devise a list of questions for national park rangers, which they can ask over e-mail to the park service, or ask in person on an actual visit to a park.

### Modify the Level:

1. Beginning students can research the locations and general features of a particular park.

2. Advanced students can design a virtual tour of a park using a presentation program (or a paper visitor's brochure).

3. Advanced students can role play park rangers and visitors. Suggest a variety of scenarios (e.g., illegal camping, bear warnings, requesting information, inclement weather warnings, etc.)

# Boomerang Beach
*Exploring Australia*

| | |
|---|---|
| **Integrated Skills:** | SPEAKING; Listening; Reading; Writing |
| **Level:** | Advanced |

**Objectives:**

*HOTS*  Students will gather and compile information about Australia.

*HOTS*  Students will negotiate for information in order to select the state/territory most appropriate to their needs.

*HOTS*  Students will evaluate presentation performances.

*HOTS*  Students will synthesize information and write a composition.

**Web site address(es):**

http://fed.gov.au/ —*Information on Australian states and territories*
➔Look for " State and Territory Government Web Sites"➔Click on state/territory name

http://fed.gov.au/emblems.htm —*Australian state/territorial symbols*
➔Scroll down to state/territory names➔Look for emblem links

**Suggested Time:** Two 50-minute sessions

**Computing Skills:** Performing a search

**Additional Resources:**
- Role cards
- VCR (optional)
- Map

# TEACHER GUIDE

| | |
|---|---|
| **Preactivity Day 1**  | **Schema Building:** <br> 1. Introduce the activity by discussing the states and territories of Australia. What do they already know about Australia? What do they think of when they hear about Australia? <br><br> 2. Ask if there are any parts of Australia students know very little about. What sort of information would they like to know about these places, particularly if they were thinking of moving there to live? <br><br> 3. Lead a discussion on what an *exposition* is and ask students if they have ever attended one. |

| **Activity Days 1–2**  | **Grouping:** <br> Groups | **Setup:** <br> Students will locate information on an Australian state or territory that would attract businesses, residents, and tourists, including that related to history, culture, recreation, taxes, education, and so on. |
|---|---|---|
| | 1. Assign a state or territory to a group, and ask each group to locate websites and extract information. Remind them of the kind of information they are looking for. <br><br> 2. Using the gathered information, each group prepares a "conference booth" for an *Annual Exposition of Australian States and Territories*. Students prepare a poster with the name of the state or territory, and emblems representing it, such as its official flag, bird, animal, and flower. <br><br> 3. Assign individual students roles to play (sample characters provided on page 58). Have them pretend they are planning to move to Australia. They are to find the state or territory that suits them the best (keeping the needs of their imaginary companion in mind as well) while attending the exposition. <br><br> 4. Distribute worksheets/rubrics for students to complete during the "exposition." <br><br> 5. Have the groups present their booths. One student remains in the booth answering questions, while the other group members (playing their roles) circulate around the "exposition" gathering information and asking questions. After 15 minutes, students switch roles. | |

| **Postactivity Day 2**  | Have each student write a paper discussing which state or territory they decided to go to and why they chose it. (Be sure to specify the required level of detail.) |
|---|---|

**Tips:** 1. Use video/pictures of an exposition as part of the preactivity to help build schema.

2. Allow students time to think of questions once the roles have been assigned.

3. Alternative: Can be done with any country, or multiple anglophone countries.

4. Additional characters can be created as necessary.

**Activity 2.5**

**Student's name:** _____ **Date:** _____

## WORKSHEET

**PART I.   Review the exposition booths of at least 4 other states or territories**
**(Mark (X) one box per line):**

| STATE/TERRITORY NAME: | Excellent | Good | Acceptable | Not Acceptable | Other Comments |
|---|---|---|---|---|---|
| Attractiveness of overall display | | | | | |
| Attractiveness of state/territory to businesses | | | | | |
| Attractiveness of state/territory to new residents | | | | | |
| Attractiveness of state/territory to tourists | | | | | |
| Information provided was clear | | | | | |
| Information provided was well organized | | | | | |
| Representatives were competent and informative | | | | | |
| **STATE/TERRITORY NAME:** | **Excellent** | **Good** | **Acceptable** | **Not Acceptable** | **Other Comments** |
| Attractiveness of overall display | | | | | |
| Attractiveness of state/territory to businesses | | | | | |
| Attractiveness of state/territory to new residents | | | | | |
| Attractiveness of state/territory to tourists | | | | | |
| Information provided was clear | | | | | |
| Information provided was well organized | | | | | |
| Representatives were competent and informative | | | | | |
| **STATE/TERRITORY NAME:** | **Excellent** | **Good** | **Acceptable** | **Not Acceptable** | **Other Comments** |
| Attractiveness of overall display | | | | | |
| Attractiveness of state/territory to businesses | | | | | |
| Attractiveness of state/territory to new residents | | | | | |
| Attractiveness of state/territory to tourists | | | | | |
| Information provided was clear | | | | | |
| Information provided was well organized | | | | | |
| Representatives were competent and informative | | | | | |
| **STATE/TERRITORY NAME:** | **Excellent** | **Good** | **Acceptable** | **Not Acceptable** | **Other Comments** |
| Attractiveness of overall display | | | | | |
| Attractiveness of state/territory to businesses | | | | | |
| Attractiveness of state/territory to new residents | | | | | |
| Attractiveness of state/territory to tourists | | | | | |
| Information provided was clear | | | | | |
| Information provided was well organized | | | | | |
| Representatives were competent and informative | | | | | |

**PART II.   Review your own conference booth**

| STATE/TERRITORY NAME: | Excellent | Good | Acceptable | Not Acceptable | Other Comments |
|---|---|---|---|---|---|
| Attractiveness of overall display | | | | | |
| Attractiveness of state/territory to businesses | | | | | |
| Attractiveness of state/territory to new residents | | | | | |
| Attractiveness of state/territory to tourists | | | | | |
| Information provided was clear | | | | | |
| Information provided was well organized | | | | | |
| Representatives were competent and informative | | | | | |

# Activity 2.5

## Further Activities:

1. Once all the groups have presented, the class will vote on the most attractive state or terriotory, the one with the best recreational opportunities, the best environmental policies, the best commercial opportunities, and so on.

2. Have students design and make a brochure highlighting the most attractive features of their state or territory.

3. Have students research Australian immigration policies and present to the class.

4. You may allow the students to examine a map and choose a state/territory for themselves.

## Modify the Level:

Beginning students can look for basic information on a state or territory, such as location, motto, flower, song, and so forth.

### Sample characters for students to play
*(photocopy and trim into sets so students can see and consider the roles of their partners)*:

| | | |
|---|---|---|
| Wang Min (married to Susan). 30 years old. Has two kids (ages 2 & 6). Works as a computer engineer. Likes rollerblading and mountain biking. | Susan (married to Wang Min). 27 years old. Has 2 kids (ages 2 & 6). Homemaker, who loves shopping, plays, concerts and opera. | Albert. 75 years old. Widowed. Retired coal miner. Likes fishing, gardening, & reading. Looking for a parttime job. |
| Mike (girlfriend is Julie). 25 years old. Works as a graphic artist. Wants to start a Master's degree in Commercial Art. Loves ethnic foods and gambling. | Julie (boyfriend is Mike). 34 years old. Corporate executive. Wants to start a family soon. Loves rock climbing and snowboarding. | Tom (best friends with Frank). 22 years old. Runs a baseball card trading company on the Internet with Frank. Enjoys meditation and Tai Chi. |
| Maria Irena (married to Alex). 64 years old. Retired store clerk. Likes swimming, knitting sweaters for her grandchildren, and going to the beach. | Alex (married to Maria Irena). 67 years old. Retired postal worker. Likes golf. His doctor recommends a warm, dry climate. | Frank (best friends with Tom). 23 years old. Runs a baseball card trading company on the Internet with Tom. Loves to kayak and play baseball. |
| Sara (sister is Caroline). 27 years old. Divorced. Works as a park ranger. Has 2 kids (9 & 12). Loves nature and almost all outdoor activities. | Caroline (sister is Sarah). 33 years old. Single. Works as a ski instructor. Loves skiing, snowboarding and hiking. Devoted to her sister's family. | Paul (married to Akiko). 42 years old. 1 child (age 5). Works as a software engineer. Loves fine restaurants, good wine, plays, and opera. |
| Eduardo (business partner is Candace). 31 years old. Married, no kids. Wife stays at home. Wants to start up an electronics firm. Loves football. | Candace (business partner is Eduardo). 32 years old. Single, 1 child (age 7). Wants to start up an electronics firm. Loves sailing on her sailboat. | Akiko (married to Paul). 41 years old. 1 child (age 5). Works as a plastic surgeon. Loves restaurants and coffee shops. Jogs every morning. |

# Language Limbo
*Debating Controversial Issues*

| | |
|---|---|
| **Integrated Skills:** | SPEAKING; Listening; Reading; Culture |
| **Level:** | Advanced |

**Objectives:**

*HOTS*    Students will gather information to support their positions on controversial issues.

*HOTS*    Students will collaborate to organize their arguments.

*HOTS*    Students will analyze, evaluate, and reconstruct their arguments.

*HOTS*    Students will debate the topic.

**Website Address(es):**    *Click the "Search" button on your browser or use any search engine*

**Suggested Time:**    Five 50-minute sessions

**Computing Skills:**    Performing a search

**Additional Resources:**    VCR (optional)

# TEACHER GUIDE

| | | |
|---|---|---|
| **Preactivity Day 1**  | **Schema Building:** <br> 1. Introduce a controversial issue and lead a class discussion (e.g., gun control, euthanasia, capital punishment, etc.) <br><br> 2. Introduce the notion of a formal debate, the role of a moderator, and the importance of the rules. | |
| **Activity Days 2– 4**  | **Grouping:** <br> Divide students into two groups: proponents and opponents (see Tip 2 following). | **Setup:** <br> In their groups, proponents and opponents collaborate to gather information to support their respective positions. |
| | 1. Decide on a topic (or allow students to choose). Assign students to the roles of opponents or proponents for that topic, and distribute worksheets. <br><br> 2. Students go to the Internet individually to gather information to support their side. They make a list of the sites visited, and summarize the content of each one in terms of *efficacy* of argument and *quality* of supporting data. Finally, they identify five supporting arguments common to most sites visited, and five less common arguments. <br><br> 3. Have students meet with the other members of their side and share what they found. They decide which members will focus on which aspects of the argument and organize their approach to the debate ahead. Students then return to the Internet to gather information to further support their assigned aspect of the discussion. <br><br> 4. Students conduct a formal debate under the guidance of a moderator. | |
| **Postactivity Day 5**  | Individual students compose a position paper on the topic covered in the debate. | |

Student's name: _____ Date:_____

## WORKSHEET

**What is the debate topic?** _____

**What is your position on this topic?**     (Circle one)     Proponent     Opponent

- **On a separate sheet of paper**, list and summarize the websites visited, note the supporting arguments, and evaluate them for quality and efficacy (how believable are the arguments found there?)

- Below, list five major arguments common to most sites visited. List five secondary arguments.

_____

_____

_____

_____

_____

_____

_____

_____

_____

_____

_____

_____

_____

_____

_____

_____

_____

_____

_____

_____

_____

_____

_____

_____

**Activity 2.6**

## Further Activities:

1. Have students switch roles and enter another round of debate.

2. Have students write a summary of their experience in the debate.

3. Have students make an oral report on a controversial issue, researching and reporting different points of view.

## Modify the Level:

Beginning/intermediate students can make a report from either the proponent's or opponent's point of view.

 **Tips:**

1. You may wish to familiarize yourself with the definition and rules of a formal debate prior to conducting the lesson.

2. For a very large class, consider dividing the class into two or three groups of proponents and opponents, each with a different debate topic. Each group conducts the debate in front of the rest of the class. The audience can then vote on the winning side.

3. Remind students to stay away from emotional or personal attacks on others. This is about the issues, not about individuals.

4. Remind students that if necessary they must argue their position in spite of their personal views on the topic.

5. You can act as moderator, or assign a mature, capable, confident student to the role.

6. Be sensitive to individual students and their cultures of origin and avoid issues that are too uncomfortable or controversial for students.

7. For the preactivity, a video of an actual debate may help introduce the topic.

# Skimming & Deep Diving:
# Reading Skills and
# Comprehension

# A Rationale & Guide for Integrating Reading into English Language Instruction

## Jeffra Flaitz

Did you read the newspaper this morning? Did you understand it? If you were asked to respond to a list of questions related to the articles you read this morning, would you receive a perfect score? Probably not, because the task would require you to remember what you read, as do most comprehension questions that follow the typical foreign language reading passage. Any number of things can impede recall, including anxiety, fatigue, and lack of interest in the material or the task. Yet we typically wait until the end of a passage to ask students if they have understood, and then assume that correct responses to our questions reflect comprehension. Moreover, it is not uncommon for teachers and textbooks to dwell on the so-called comprehension questions rather than on developing reading skill. How accurate a measure of comprehension are such questions, particularly if phrased in multiple-choice or true/false formats? Furthermore, even if the questions are well phrased, both teachers and students tend to be uncomfortable with anything less than 100 percent comprehension of a text, yet few of us could lay claim to that level of comprehension and recall in our first language. What we are failing to teach is the far more important skill of reading, which involves active interpretations and estimations of contextual and lexical clues, including related text and images, word and morpheme frequency, as well as the reader's background and cultural knowledge.

In other words, reading is complex. There are many different kinds and levels of cognitive processing involved. It is important, too, to recognize it as a process. As such, it requires dynamic interaction between the individual and the text, plus a good deal of effort, practice, and awareness of how to become a better reader.

What is meant by *dynamic interaction*? An example will illustrate. Pick up the finance page of the newspaper. For most of us, articles in this area are often incomprehensible because of the use of specialized vocabulary and our lack of familiarity with the subject matter. As you read the headlines, you immediately begin to scan your memory for familiar information or personal experience related to one of the topics. You are using *top-down processing* to access *schemata*, or knowledge structures, that you have at your disposal anytime you encounter a new experience. Secure that you have had some exposure to the chosen topic, you let your eyes run quickly down the column of text, picking out familiar names, getting a sense of the overall gist of the article, and sizing up the actual reading task. You glance quickly at the adjacent photograph and read the next line of text, framing it within your background knowledge structures. Here is the word *fiduciary*. It is unfamiliar, so you make a quick mental note of it, and move on. You subconsciously trust that you will understand its meaning as you progress through the article; you also consider the possibility that the word in and of itself may not be critical to your understanding of the text as a whole.

The article is written in the past tense, so you assume that it provides an account of an event that has already taken place. Moreover, you assume, and find, that the account unfolds in a predictable way; the main event, a merger between two large corporations, appears in the first paragraph, and details appear in subsequent paragraphs. This familiar organizational plan helps you to anticipate information that is yet to come. Your eyes now move back up to the photograph, two smiling executives standing in front of a dozen microphones and reporters. This confirms your hypothesis that the merger was deemed not only "good" but also important. Most of all, the result of your dynamic interaction with the text has increased your ability to comprehend and enjoy the reading task. Notice, too, that your objective was neither to gain something meaningful from the text (and not necessarily learn the meaning of the word *fiduciary*) nor to remember tomorrow what you read today.

Teaching students to be good readers is no easy task, as reading requires multiple skills, such as scanning, skimming, recognizing, predicting, and extracting relevant information. The task may be made somewhat lighter by choosing texts that engage and interest students, and that are appropriate to their cognitive and linguistic levels. As teachers it is up to us to not only cultivate in our students the complex skills required to read efficiently and effectively, but to motivate them by choosing meaningful and interesting materials that engage their interest and inspire them to read increasingly complex and challenging texts. Reading is the focus of the lessons in this chapter, and additional skills are integrated into the activities.

# TEACHING TIPS FOR READING

## Modeling:

♦ Show your students how to read by thinking aloud as you read a sample text for them.

♦ Remember that reading aloud is essentially a pronunciation exercise for the reader.

## Preparation:

♦ Access students' schemata by asking questions on their knowledge of the topic. Build schemata with discussions, pictures, videos, exploration, and so on.

♦ Ask your students to consider the whole text before they begin to read in terms of length, difficulty, interest, and general content.

♦ Draw students' attention to any pictures, icons, bold or italicized words, and subheadings.

## Negotiation:

♦ Allow students to express their opinions about the text in terms of difficulty, interest, and so on.

♦ Give students an opportunity to choose from a selection of texts or allow them to suggest texts for reading.

♦ Read together in class and orally practice the skills (hypothesizing, inferencing, confirming, questioning, predicting, drawing on cultural and linguistic schemata) needed for successful independent reading.

♦ Teach your students through skill building to rely more on themselves than on you.

## Expectations:

♦ Make sure texts are not always processed in exactly the same way, since predictability can dampen students' enthusiasm.

♦ Provide traditional "end-of-text" questions before the reading assignment is given to downplay the role of memorization.

♦ Introduce the notion of tolerance of ambiguity. The expectations of 100 percent comprehension of a text will likely lead to frustration.

## Motivation:

♦ Encourage USSR (Uninterrupted Sustained Silent Reading). Do not "ban" any topic or type of reading material.

♦ Reward efforts to read for pleasure outside of class.

♦ Schedule DEAR (Drop Everything and Read) time into your curriculum.

## Level:

♦ Select texts that are neither too easy nor too difficult.

♦ Give students an opportunity to feel both challenged and successful.

♦ Emphasize interest and relevance in the selection of texts, rather than level of difficulty.

♦ Remember that authentic material has more potential for success than a contrived text.

♦ Have students read demanding text selectively, focusing on excepts or facets of the text rather than on the entire document.

# READING TIPS FOR STUDENTS

◆ Read, read, read for pleasure.

- comic books
- fashion magazines
- novels
- academic texts
- opinion/editorial pieces in the newspaper

◆ Try to read without the aid of a dictionary.

◆ Use the title, subheadings, pictures, words in bold or italics, and so on to help you get an idea of what the text will be about.

◆ Ask yourself questions *before* you begin to read:

- What do I want to learn from reading this text?
- What do I think this reading will be about?
- What kind of person probably wrote this text?
- How do I think the author of the text will present her ideas?
- What kind of organizational plan do I expect to find?
- Will I enjoy reading this piece?

◆ Ask yourself questions *while* you read:

- What is the main idea?
- What do I expect to read in the next section of the text?
- How can I figure out the meaning of a word I don't recognize?
- Do I really need my dictionary?
- Is the word important?
- What part of speech is this word?
- Can I identify any of its affixes?
- Does it look like a word in my language or a word that I have seen before in the target language?

◆ Try to summarize the text quickly in your head before moving on to another activity.

◆ Don't translate as you read.

◆ Believe in your ability to read well, but don't expect to understand everything you read. Not even native speakers can do that!

# Save the Manatees
### *Discovering an Endangered Species*

| | |
|---|---|
| **Integrated Skills:** | READING; Speaking; Writing |

| | |
|---|---|
| **Level:** | Beginning |

**Objectives:**

- Students will extract information about manatees from a written text.

*HOTS* Students will draw inferences from the information they obtain.

*HOTS* Students will discuss the meanings of selected words.

**Website Address(es):**

http://www.geocities.com/Heartland/5960/manatee.html
—*Information on manatees*

http://www.homesafe.com/manatee/manatee-facts.html
—*Information on manatees*

**Suggested Time:** Two 50-minute sessions

**Additional Resources:**
- World map
- Dictionary (optional)

# TEACHER GUIDE

| | |
|---|---|
| **Preactivity Day 1**  | **Schema Building:** <br> 1. Show pictures of endangered animals. Describe and name these animals. Ask students what these animals have in common, and introduce the subject of endangered species. <br><br> 2. Show pictures of manatees and ask students what they know about them. Add that they are sometimes referred to as "sea cows," and that sailors originally mistook them for mermaids. |

| | | |
|---|---|---|
| **Activity Day 1**  | **Grouping:** <br> Part I:  Individual <br> Part II: <br> Pairs/Groups | **Setup:** <br> Students will read about manatees, extract information, and make inferences using this information. |
| | Part I: <br> 1. Distribute the worksheets and have students go to one of the provided websites. They then complete the worksheet. <br><br> Part II: <br> 2. Pair or group students and have them share their findings. | |

| | |
|---|---|
| **Postactivity Day 2**  | 1. Have students individually return to their chosen website. Have them scan the text and choose five intriguing words they do not know (see Tip 3 following). <br><br> 2. Put students back into groups and ask them to discuss the words they chose. Each group selects one word they find difficult, and write it on the board. Have the rest of the class attempt to guess the meaning of the word. |

**Tips:**

1. Be certain to use a variety of animal pictures in the preactivity, including mammals, reptiles, birds, fish, and so on.

2. Animal pictures may be downloaded from the Internet.

3. Encourage students to choose words they think are important. They can share why they picked those words. In addition, parameters may be given to the students to control their word choices, such as number of syllables, frequency of occurrence, and so on.

Student's name: _____Date:_____

## WORKSHEET

**True or False (Circle One)**

   1. Manatees breathe air.                        True          False

   2. Manatees eat meat.                         True          False

   3. Manatees live on land.                     True          False

   4. Manatees can give birth to 3 to 4 babies at one time.     True          False

   5. Manatees live in lakes.                    True          False

   6. Manatees are gentle creatures.            True          False

   7. Manatees are endangered because of humans.      True          False

   8. Why must people protect manatees?  _____

_____

   9. How can we protect manatees?   _____

_____

   10. How long do manatees live? _____

   11. Where do manatees live?    _____

   12. How big is a manatee?     _____

**Activity 3.1**

**Further Activities:**

1. Take students to a zoo or an aquarium and find endangered animals.

2. Distribute photocopies of a world map. Have students mark the locations where manatees are found, and indicate migration patterns and/or population estimates.

**Modify the Level:**

1. Intermediate students can gather pictures of endangered marine mammals. Have students compare the ways in which the survival of these animals is threatened, in addition to current population estimates. Finally, ask them to discuss what can be done to save these animals.

2. Advanced students can work as a class to research a multitude of aspects concerning a single endangered species (remaining numbers, habitat, how to save them, etc.). Results can be compiled into a class project to be displayed at the school.

3. Advanced students can be individually assigned specific endangered species to research in depth and report on.

# Menus to Go-Go
## *Creating Original Menus*

| | |
|---|---|
| **Integrated Skills:** | READING; Speaking; Culture |
| **Level:** | Beginning |

**Objectives:**

- Students will scan restaurant menus.

 *HOTS*    Students will sort and select dishes according to a list of specifications.

*HOTS*    Students will compare and discuss their findings.

*HOTS*    Students will create original menus.

 **Website Address(es):**

http://www.xlibris.co.uk/latuskes —*Menu site*
➔Click on "The menu"

http://www.tullysrest.com —*Menu site*
➔Click on "The menu"

http://www.jaspers-restaurant.co.uk —*Menu site*
➔Click on "Menus"➔Scroll down and click

**Suggested Time:** Three 50-minute sessions

# TEACHER GUIDE

| | |
|---|---|
| **Preactivity Day 1**  | **Schema Building:** <br> 1. Introduce the activity by asking students what they do when organizing a party. <br><br> 2. List food categories on the board (vegetables, seafood, desserts, etc.) and have students brainstorm food vocabulary they already know. <br><br> 3. Next, discuss the courses typically included in a formal dinner and the kinds of foods that would be eaten during each. <br><br> 4. Ask students what they would do if some of their guests were not able to eat all types of foods. <br><br> 5. Ask students what they would do if they had no time to prepare food for the party. Who else could they ask to prepare the food? |

| | | |
|---|---|---|
| **Activity Day 2**  | **Grouping:** <br> Part I: <br> Individual <br> Part II:  Groups | **Setup:** <br> Students will look for dishes from a variety of restaurant menus in order to compose a complete meal that will please *all* their guests. |
| | **Part I:** <br> 1. Distribute the worksheets, and have students access the provided websites. Students examine available menus and, by process of elimination, choose dishes that will satisfy all of their guests (see Tip following). <br><br> **Part II:** <br> 2. Assign students to groups, and have them discuss their reasons for choosing certain dishes over others (needs of their guests, flavor, cost, etc.). They must reach an agreement as a group and establish a final list of dishes to serve at a party. | |

| | |
|---|---|
| **Postactivity Day 3**  | Ask the groups to produce a menu that includes an *à la carte* breakdown of selections by courses, with two to three options available for each course. They should be certain to include foods that would satisfy people with varying needs and wants. |

 **Tips:** If there are as many computers available as there are students, then the entire activity can be done in groups. In this case, each student within a group can be assigned to one party guest and look for a list of dishes appropriate to that guest.

**Student's name:** _____ **Date:**_____

## WORSHEET

### DESIGNING A MENU

**Think about your friends (examples):**
- Jeff is allergic to shellfish (clams, oysters, shrimp, etc.)
- Caroline cannot eat eggs.
- Bob does not like onions or garlic.
- Lauren cannot digest dairy products (milk, cream, cheese, etc.)
- Monica does not eat red meat.

**Salad** _____

Ingredients: _____

_____

**Soup** _____

Ingredients: _____

_____

**Main Dish** _____

Ingredients: _____

_____

**Side Dish** _____

Ingredients: _____

_____

**Dessert** _____

Ingredients: _____

_____

**Activity 3.2**

## Further Activities:

1. Pair members from different groups and seat them back to back so that they may hold a mock telephone conversation. They should play the roles of party planner and restaurant owner and pretend to place an order for the food they've chosen.

2. Students can suggest additional dishes to add to the party menu. Proposals can be considered by the group (taking into account the parameters of the activity) and decided on together.

## Modify the Level:

1. Intermediate students can pretend that they will open a restaurant. They should research and create a menu for the kind of food they will serve. This can be followed by having students role play visiting and ordering at their peers' restaurants.

2. Advanced students can work together to create a calorie-conscious menu.

3. Advanced students can role play as food critics. They can pretend to sample a variety of dishes and evaluate them for taste, presentation, and so forth.

# London Luau
*Uncovering London's Treasures*

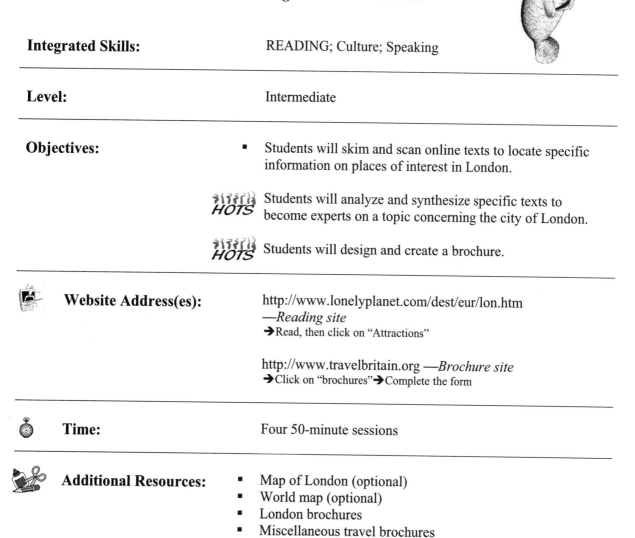

| | |
|---|---|
| **Integrated Skills:** | READING; Culture; Speaking |
| **Level:** | Intermediate |

**Objectives:**

- Students will skim and scan online texts to locate specific information on places of interest in London.

*HOTS* Students will analyze and synthesize specific texts to become experts on a topic concerning the city of London.

*HOTS* Students will design and create a brochure.

**Website Address(es):**

http://www.lonelyplanet.com/dest/eur/lon.htm
—*Reading site*
➔Read, then click on "Attractions"

http://www.travelbritain.org —*Brochure site*
➔Click on "brochures"➔Complete the form

**Time:** Four 50-minute sessions

**Additional Resources:**

- Map of London (optional)
- World map (optional)
- London brochures
- Miscellaneous travel brochures

# TEACHER GUIDE

| | |
|---|---|
| **Preactivity Day 1**  | **Schema Building:** <br> 1. Ask students what activities they would like to do if they went on a trip. <br> 2. Ask students what comes to mind when they think about London. Ask if anyone has ever been there before. <br> 3. Together, locate London on a world map. Look at where it is situated in the United Kingdom. <br> 4. Next, look together at a detailed map of the city (see Tip 1). What would students like to do there? <br> 5. Pass around copies of tourist brochures to students (see Tip 2). Discuss together what a brochure is for, and what kinds of information one should contain. |
| **Activity Day 2**  | **Grouping:** <br> Part I: Individual <br> Part II: Small groups <br><br> **Setup:** <br> Students will gather information for a scavenger hunt and will become experts on one of the topics on the list. <br><br> Part I: <br> 1. Distribute worksheets and have students go to the website, read, and gather answers for a scavenger hunt (answers appear on page 80). <br><br> Part II: <br> 2. Once the scavenger hunt is complete, go over the worksheet. <br> 3. Assign to each group, or have groups choose, one of the topics from the hunt. <br> 4. Students return to the Web to research, gather details and become "experts" on their topics. |
| **Postactivity Days 3-4**  | 1. Still in their groups, students create a brochure on the place of interest they were assigned to research in depth. Brochures may be created with a word processor, and once completed, copies should be made for everyone in the class. <br> 2. Have students read through one another's brochures, and formulate appropriate questions to ask the "experts." <br> 3. Next, have each group act, in turn, as an expert panel to answer their classmates' questions. <br> 4. Finally, using one of the provided websites, have students return to the Internet and request an authentic brochure on London. |

 **Tips:**

1. A city map can be found on the Internet. Use "London map" as search engine keyword.

2. Order brochures from a British Tourist office, via the Internet at http://www.travelbritain.org, or pick some up at a local travel agency.

3. Students can divide the scavenger hunt task among group members if time is a constraint.

Student's name: _____ Date: _____

## WORSHEET

**ANSWER THE FOLLOWING QUESTIONS:**

1. Which museum is the most prestigious in the world?

   _____

2. Where can you find Egyptian-style catacombs?

   _____

3. Where would you go to get your ear pierced?

   _____

4. What do the Beefeaters guard?

   _____

5. Where in London can you go to see one of the world's most impressive art collections?

   _____

6. Where can you find the London Zoo, a mosque, and an open-air theatre?

   _____

7. In which former vegetable garden can you now shop in expensive stores ?

   _____

8. In what season do Londoners celebrate Guy Fawkes Day?

   _____

9. Where did the king go hunting?

   _____

10. Where can you check to see what time it is?

    _____

11. Where can you buy records and clothing from the 1960s?

    _____

12. Which of London's famous buildings is constructed in the Gothic-Revival style and has a grand, cathedral-like main entrance?

    _____

**Activity 3.3**

## Further Activities:

1. Using their classmates' brochures, have students plan a one- to three-day itinerary for a visit to London.

2. As a class, students set up a mock travel agency to be visited by students from other classes. They may display their brochures on tables and answer questions.

3. Show a travel video of London, or take a trip to London.

## Modify the Level:

1. Beginning students can do a modified scavenger hunt, searching only for items mentioned explicitly in the text.

2. Advanced students can create a multimedia presentation of London tourist attractions.

3. Advanced students can create a multimedia presentation of other English-speaking places they would like to visit.

## Answers to the worksheet:

| | | |
|---|---|---|
| 1. The British Museum | 5. The National Gallery | 9. Hyde Park |
| 2. Highgate Cemetery | 6. Regent's Park | 10. Big Ben |
| 3. Kensington Market | 7. Covent Garden | 11. Camden Market |
| 4. The Tower of London | 8. Fall/Autumn | 12. The Natural History Museum |

# Legend of Atlantis
*Analyzing Native American Legends*

| | |
|---|---|
| **Integrated Skills:** | READING; Culture; Speaking; Listening |
| **Level:** | Intermediate |
| **Objectives:** | *HOTS* Students will analyze the content of a Native American short story. |
| | *HOTS* Students will retell their short story in their own words. |
| | ▪ Students will identify the principal metaphors and similes. |
| **Website Address(es):** | http://pages.tca.net/martikw/legendke.html —*Story site* |
| | http://www.looksmart.com/eus1/eus53706/eus53710/ eus266442/eus280841/ —*Links to stories* |
| | http://www.kstrom.net/isk/stories/myths.html—*Links to stories* |
| | http://www.lausd.k12.ca.us/lausd/resources/shakespeare/ Literary.Terms.Menu.html—*Explanation of literary terms* ➔Click to read about metaphors and similes |
| **Suggested Time:** | Three 50-minute sessions |
| **Additional Resources:** | Pictures or movie clip of Native Americans (optional) |

**Activity 3.4**

| | |
|---|---|
| **Preactivity Day 1**  | **Schema Building:** 1. Introduce the concepts of *metaphor* and *simile* by offering examples to students, such as, respectively; <br> *People in glass houses should not throw stones.* <br> or <br> *Her hands were as cold as ice.* <br> Put students into groups and have them discuss your examples, interpret their meanings and derive a definition for *metaphor* and for *simile*. Once the groups have shared their ideas with the class, discuss how metaphors and similes convey embedded meanings, and why they are used. <br><br> 2. Read aloud to the class a fable you select. Work as a class to identify the main ideas, the metaphors, and the similes. <br><br> 3. Ask students if they have ever told stories with a group of friends or family members (see Tip 1). |
| **Activity Day 2**  | **Grouping:** Individual     **Setup:** Students will read a Native American legend, identify the metaphors and similes, and analyze the story. <br><br> 1. Distribute worksheets. Have students access the provided websites and search for a legend to read. <br><br> 2. Ask students to write a summary of the legend they read. |
| **Postactivity Day 3**  | 1. In small groups, students recall the legends they read and tell them to their partners (see Tip 2). <br><br> 2. When finished, students share the metaphors and similes from their worksheets and discuss them in terms of cultural relevance. |

**Tips:**  1. If possible, show pictures or a movie clip of Native Americans (or any group) sitting together and telling stories.

2. When grouping the students, attempt to verify that they have read a variety of legends.

3. Be certain that students understand that they are to *retell* the legend they found, and not read it verbatim to their partners.

**Student's name:** _____**Date:**_____

## WORKSHEET

**NATIVE AMERICAN LEGENDS**     Locate and read a legend. Read it once to get the main idea, then read it a second or third time and answer these questions:

1.  Website where you found your legend:

   **http://** _____

2.  What is the title of the legend?

   _____

3.  Can you find the author of the legend?
    If not, why do you think this is?

   _____

   _____

4.  What Native American tribe does this legend come from?

   _____

5.  What is the topic of the story?

   _____

6.  What are the major ideas developed?

   _____

   _____

   _____

   _____

7.  What are the main metaphors used in the story and why do you think they are important?

   _____

   _____

   _____

   _____

8.  What are the main similes used in the legend, and how do they contribute to the story?

   _____

   _____

   _____

   _____

**Activity 3.4**

**Further Activities:**

1. Students can work on groups to role play a legend of their choice.

2. Students can tell a legend or story from their own culture.

3. Students may draw a comic book–style representation of a legend or story.

**Modify the Level:**

1. Beginning students can work in groups to interpret a short fable and identify its metaphors and similes.

2. Advanced students can invent a legend of their own, incorporating metaphors and similes.

# Seasick

*Identifying Illnesses from Their Symptoms*

| | |
|---|---|
| **Integrated Skills:** | READING; Speaking; Listening |
| **Level:** | Advanced |
| **Objectives:** | ▪ Students will identify an illness based on a set of symptoms. |
| *HOTS* | Students will compare and correlate descriptions of illnesses with descriptions of symptoms. |
| *HOTS* | Students will discuss their findings and reach a consensus on a diagnosis. |
| **Website Address(es):** | http://onhealth.webmd.com/ —*Healthcare site* ➔Click on "Symptom Checker" ➔Scroll down and click "General Symptoms" ➔Read, search, and click until a diagnosis can be made |
| **Suggested Time:** | Four 50-minute sessions |
| **Computing Skills:** | Performing a search |

**TEACHER GUIDE**

| | |
|---|---|
| **Preactivity Day 1**<br> | **Schema Building:**<br>1. Ask students if any of them have been sick lately. Ask volunteers to explain their symptoms without naming the illness. Build a list on the board (i.e., runny nose, stuffy head, sore or scratchy throat, nausea, fever, body aches, sneezing, coughing, phlegm, etc.)<br>Next, ask the class if they can identify the illness just described.<br><br>2. Have students brainstorm for symptoms and add to the list on the board (supplying new words where necessary).<br><br>**Modeling:**<br>1. Pass out the preactivity reading passage on the flu, and have students read and discuss it and attempt to identify the illness involved.<br><br>2. Students acess the provided website. In the search field on the web page, have students enter the name of the illness they believe is causing the symptoms described in the reading passage.<br><br>3. Discuss findings as a class. Reach a consensus on a probable cause of illness. |
| **Activity Days 2–3**<br> | **Grouping:** Individual and small groups.    **Setup:** Given a description of symptoms, students will search the Internet for corresponding illnesses, their causes, and their treatments.<br><br>1. Divide the class into three groups, and give each group one of the three provided reading passages.<br><br>2. Students read the passages then, as a group, discuss, agree on, and list three to four possible diseases they believe correspond to the symptoms presented therein (see Tip 3 for the answers).<br><br>3. Ask students to individually search the provided website (or to do an Internet search) and read to determine the cause of the illness that best matches the symptomatic information provided in the passage. Students may need to read several texts until they locate an illness that best explains the symptoms.<br><br>4. Have students reconvene in groups and discuss their findings until they reach a consensus on a diagnosis.<br><br>5. Students then return individually to the Internet and locate and list (1) treatments, (2) preventative measures, and (3) causes.<br><br>6. Ask students to rejoin their respective groups and finalize their analyses of the causes, treatment, and prevention of the illness in question. |
| **Postactivity Day 4**<br> | Have students creatively present their findings to the class in the form of role play, by acting out the roles of patient, doctor, nurse, relatives, and so on. Encourage them to incorporate as much of the information they found as possible. |

---

## Reading Passage - Preactivity

Eloise

Yesterday, Eloise went home exhausted. She went to bed with a pounding headache and a sensation of dizziness. She tossed and turned all night long. This morning she woke up fatigued. Her body ached all over, she had chills, and her throat was sore. She took her temperature and discovered that she had a fever of 102°F.

---

## Reading Passage I

George

Yesterday, George had dinner with Jane at a small restaurant called "Chicken-Rite." During the night he began to feel nauseated. Later his stomach hurt and he developed a rash all over his body. This morning, his symptoms were worse, and he began vomiting and experiencing diarrhea. By the early afternoon, George felt very dehydrated. An hour later, Jane called to say that she could not meet with him that evening because she had a fever, abdominal pains, and was vomiting as well.

---

## Reading Passage II

Matthew

Matthew doesn't feel well at all. He woke up feeling nauseated and feverish. He normally has a hearty appetite, but today he doesn't feel like eating anything. Earlier in the day, his stomach was tender above the navel, and he was experiencing cramps. By afternoon, the pain had extended down into his lower right abdomen.

---

## Reading Passage III

Jerry

Jerry leads a very stressful life. He frequently feels nauseated and bloated. Lately, he has been feeling a sharp, burning pain in his stomach. The pain is very high up in his abdomen and it keeps him awake at night. He has heartburn regularly and vomits occasionally.

**Activity 3.5**

**Further Activities:**

1. Students research an illness and create a "reading passage" modeled after those found in the activity.

2. Have students investigate alternative medicines to treat the illness in question (such as homeopathic remedies, acupuncture, aromatherapy, etc.), and present them to their groups.

3. Have students search for additional sites similar to the one they used in the activity.

4. Have students search the Internet for the names and activities of various medical organizations, such as general associations and those concerned with specific diseases.

**Modify the Level:**

1. Intermediate students can be assigned specific symptoms to search for on the provided website.

2. Intermediate students can individually read the "What is it?" section on the provided website and report their findings.

 **Tips:**  1.  You may devise and distribute additional reading passages if desired.

      2.  If time is an issue, steps 5 and 6 of the activity can be done as homework.

      3.  Correct identifications of the illnesses:
*Passage I—food poisoning; Passage II—appendicitis; Passage III—peptic ulcer*

# Making Waves
*Following Instructions To Construct a Website*

| | |
|---|---|
| **Integrated Skills:** | READING; Writing; Speaking; Culture |
| **Level:** | Advanced |

**Objectives:**

- Students will identify common HTML coding tags.

- Students will interpret and follow instructions online.

*HOTS* Students will experiment with HTML code to construct a simple web page.

**Website Address(es):**

http://www.voyager.co.nz/~bsimpson/html.htm — *Instructions for creating a website*

http://webopedia.internet.com —*Encyclopedia for Web-related terms*

**Suggested Time:** Four 50-minute sessions

**Software Requirements:** Text editor (i.e., *Notepad* for *Windows*® for PCs or *AppleWorks*® for Mac OS)

**Activity 3.6**                    **TEACHER GUIDE**

| | |
|---|---|
| **Preactivity Day 1**  | **Schema Building:** <br> 1. Introduce the activity by asking students what a *website* is. Then narrow the topic down to the concept of *homepage*. <br><br> 2. Brainstorm with students how websites are designed, and what sort of information is posted on them. <br><br> 3. Ask students if they know what *HTML* means and what it is used for (see Tip 2). Be certain they also understand the term *tag*. <br><br> 4. Show a few examples of homepages (you can locate several at http://geocities.com/home. Type "personal" in the search field, and click *search*). As you look at the homepages together, make a chart of the design features within the sites that students would and would not want to imitate. |

| | | |
|---|---|---|
| **Activity Days 2–3** | **Grouping:** <br> Pairs | **Setup:** <br> Explain that students will follow online instructions to build (create) their personal web site or homepage. |

| | |
|---|---|
| **Activity Days 2–3** | 1. Put students in pairs and distribute the worksheets. Have students access one of the provided instruction sites. <br><br> 2. Ask students to fill out Part I of the worksheet in order to find specific HTML tags, which will allow them to build their homepages. (Answers are on page 92.) <br><br> 3. Using the text editors on their computers, students create a web page corresponding to the layout in Part II of their worksheet. Students must save their work as an HTML file (filename.html) in their text editor, and open it from their browser window (open file, browse to locate the HTML file, and open). The file should be displayed as shown on Part II of the worksheet. Note that students may need to toggle back and forth between the browser and the text editor until their pages are correctly displayed. Students must save after each new change, and then refresh or reload the page in the browser. |
| **Post Activity Day 4** | 1. Ask students to create their own individual homepages (this can be assigned as homework). <br><br> 2. Have students present their websites to their peers, explaining the different steps they followed during the construction of their site and the particular difficulties they encountered. |

  **Tips:**  1. You might want to use students with high computer skills or students who have already created a website to help their less skilled peers. You may also find assistance from your school's media specialist.

2. *HTML* is a special computer language used to write web pages. It stands for *Hypertext Mark-Up Language*. It is easy to use and should pose no problem to your students. A tutorial for HTML tags is available on both provided websites.

Students' names: _____ Date:_____

WORSHEET

**Part I.** Find the following codes (tags) in the provided website (the first one has been done for you as an example):

1. Tag to begin an HTML page*:*  _____*<HTML>*_____

2. Tag to end an HTML page:  _____

3. Tags (beginning and ending) to center text:  _____  _____

4. Tags (beginning and ending)  for the largest size of text :  _____  _____

5. Tag to start a new line:  _____

6. Tags (beginning and ending) to bold text:  _____  _____

7. Tag to draw a horizontal line in the text:  _____

8. Tags (beginning and ending) to title the page:  _____  _____

9. Tag to start a new paragraph:  _____

10. Tag to import a picture:  _____

11. Tags (beginning and ending) to write the content of the homepage:

  _____  _____

**Part II.**  Follow the instructions given on the assigned website for creating each line of your homepage. Your homepage should look like this:

# (Student's name) and (Student's name)'s Homepage

How do you like our first homepage?

## We love it!

Here is our dream car (maybe).

(Red<br>sports car<br>here)

**Activity 3.6**

**Further Activities:**

1. Have students write an individual report on the problems they encountered while constructing their website and on the lessons they learned.

2. Have students go back to their homepages and troubleshoot and enhance their work.

3. If server space is available, students can publish their homepages on the Web. (**Warning:** once published on the Web, the information displayed on the homepage is available to anyone. Caution students regarding the potential dangers of disclosing information of a personal nature on the Web).

**Answers to Part I of the worksheet**

| | | | |
|---|---|---|---|
| 1. Tag to begin an HTML page | <HTML> | 7. Tag to draw a horizontal line | <HR> |
| 2. Tag to end an HTML page | </HTML> | 8. Tags to title the page | <TITLE> </TITLE> |
| 3. Tags to center text | <CENTER> </CENTER> | 9. Tag to start a new paragraph | <P> |
| 4. Tag to produce the largest text | <H1> </H1> | 10. Tag to import a picture | <IMG SRC="car.gif"> |
| 5. Tag to start a new line | <BR> | 11. Tags to write the content | <BODY> </BODY> |
| 6. Tags to bold text | <B> </B> | | |

# Write a Wave:
# Developing Writing Skills

# A Rationale & Guide for Integrating Writing into English Language Instruction

## Wei Zhu

In conventional ordering of second-language skills, writing often comes later in both teaching and learning, after listening, speaking, and reading. This perhaps speaks to the perceived importance and difficulty of writing. While listening and speaking skills are essential for effective communication in many situations, writing constitutes another powerful communication tool, allowing second-language learners to perform a variety of language tasks, ranging from leaving a note for a friend to answering an essay question on an exam or preparing a research report. The lessons in this chapter center on writing, while simultaneously integrating other skills.

Writing is a difficult skill to acquire. Part of the difficulty stems from the fact that the audience the writer is addressing is typically not physically present. Consequently, the writer does not have the kind of immediate feedback needed to assess the effectiveness of the communication. Writing in the first language is already challenging, and second-language writers face an even greater challenge as they must express themselves using syntactic and rhetorical devices in a language they are still learning.

The good news is that there is much that teachers can do to help second-language learners develop writing skills. Teachers can and should address issues of grammar and vocabulary, but they can also play a very important role in helping students acquire other skills and knowledge essential for successful writing, including understanding how audience and purpose shape writing. Teachers can also help students better grasp the nature of the writing process and develop strategies for increased effectiveness. For example, students can learn that they need to focus on ideas and not be distracted by sentence-level concerns (e.g., grammar, word choice, and punctuation) during the early stages of writing. Sentence-level concerns can be addressed more effectively at the editing stages after more global issues (e.g., content and organization) have been considered.

Revision is key to improved writing. This means that students need time to compose their drafts and receive feedback on their writing, either from the teacher and/or their peers. Ideally, this editing should convey to students how successful they have been in achieving their communication goals. Feedback on grammar, word choice, and punctuation can be provided when students are ready to edit their work, allowing for contextualized grammar instruction.

Providing students with meaningful and relevant writing tasks can help motivate them, as well as see that there is a real purpose for writing. In addition, students can benefit from interesting and pertinent readings, since reading not only provides input in terms of content, but also allows students to internalize good models for writing. For example, students can read a passage, discuss it in class, and then write an essay discussing their position on a particular issue raised in the passage. When using reading to prepare students for writing, instructors can draw students' attention to the content as well as to rhetorical form and language use.

Second-language writing instruction should be approached with an understanding of the nature of the writing process and the written products, and an understanding of students' needs as writers, as well as a willingness to address students' needs individually.

# TEACHING TIPS FOR WRITING

**Modeling:**

♦ Be a good model; write with your students; share your writing with them; model writing strategies.

**Preparation:**

♦ Help students generate topics through activities such as brainstorming and listing.

♦ With assigned topics, help students generate ideas through small-group and class discussions.

♦ Teach composition strategies.

♦ Help students understand their audience and purpose for writing.

♦ Raise students' awareness of rhetorical form through reading activities.

**Process:**

♦ Provide students with feedback on drafts.

♦ Train students to be effective evaluators of peer writing.

♦ Help students monitor and evaluate their own writing.

♦ Teach revision and editing strategies.

**Expectations:**

♦ Keep in mind that the early steps of the writing process should be devoted to content and organization, not error-free writing.

♦ Be aware that second-language learners bring different levels of writing experience from their first language. Provide individualized guidance.

**Motivation:**

♦ Allow students to select their own topics whenever possible.

♦ When assigning topics, make sure that they are meaningful and relevant.

♦ Respond to student writing as an interested reader.

♦ Provide students with opportunities to "publish" their writing in a variety of formats.

♦ Help students become confident in themselves as writers.

**Level:**

♦ Keep in mind that students' language proficiency itself does not always determine writing success.

♦ Students at lower levels of proficiency can start to write.

# WRITING TIPS FOR STUDENTS

◆ Plan before you write.

◆ Focus on ideas once you start writing; don't stop often to check grammar or spelling.

◆ Keep your audience (the intended reader) and purpose (why you are writing) in mind.

◆ Seek feedback on your writing.

◆ Try to be a critical reader of your own writing.

◆ Revise (focusing on ideas and organization) as much as you can.

◆ Edit your writing carefully.

◆ Allow time for your writing.

◆ Be aware of your habits as a writer and use appropriatestrategies.

◆ Read as much as you can and pay attention to the organization of the text.

◆ Practice, practice, practice!

# Message in a Bottle
*Composing and Sending E-cards*

| | |
|---|---|
| **Integrated Skills:** | WRITING; Reading; Culture |
| **Level:** | Beginning |
| **Objectives:** | ▪ Students will discuss the custom of exchanging cards. |
| | ▪ Students will identify on what occasions to write cards. |
| | *HOTS* Students will compile expressions and phrases commonly used in writing and exchanging "thank-you" cards. |
| | *HOTS* Students will compose and send a "thank-you" card. |
| | *HOTS* Students will generate their own cards for a special occasion. |
| **Website Address(es):** | http://www4.bluemountain.com —*E-card site* |
| | http://www.care2.com/ —*E-card site*<br>➔Register for an account before entering the site |
| | http://cards.amazon.com —*E-card site* |
| **Suggested Time:** | Three 50-minute sessions |
| **Computing Skills:** | E-mailing |
| **Additional Resources:** | ▪ E-mail accounts for students<br>▪ Model "thank-you" card (optional) |

# TEACHER GUIDE

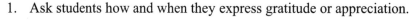

| **Preactivity Day 1** | **Schema Building:** |
|---|---|
| | 1. Ask students how and when they express gratitude or appreciation. |
| | 2. Talk about the custom of exchanging cards. Show an actual "thank-you" card to the students. Ask students if they have a similar custom in their country(-ies). |
| | 3. Have the students brainstorm the occasions when they might need to send a "thank-you" card (i.e., thanking someone for their help, a gift, or an invitation). |
| | 4. Discuss the vocabulary typically used in "thank-you" cards, such as *appreciate*, *grateful*, and so on. |

| **Activity Day 2** | **Grouping:** Individual | **Setup:** Students will access electronic greeting cards (e-cards), explore expressions, and compose their own cards. |
|---|---|---|
| | 1. Distribute worksheets and have students go to a website that offers electronic greeting cards. (If they use www.bluemountain.com, they go to the "Every Day" section and click on "Thank You.") | |
| | 2. Students read several cards at the site and record at least five expressions and phrases on Part I of their worksheets. | |
| | 3. Based on what they read, have students complete Part II of the worksheet with brief phrases appropriate to the respective situations. | |
| | 4. Next, ask students to pick one card, which they will fill out. (Be certain to help students with difficult vocabulary.) They must add two to three phrases of their own. | |
| | 5. Ask students to e-mail cards to other students in the class. (They should send a copy of their cards to you as well.) | |

| **Postactivity Day 3** | Have students create their own, handmade card (using software, paper and pen, etc.) for another occasion, which they should send to the recipient of their choice. (They may wish to view the cards at the website again to look for vocabulary and phrases.) |
|---|---|

 **Tips:**

1. You may wish to distribute a list of students' e-mail addresses.

2. If e-mail is unavailable, students may print the cards and pass them to one another in person.

3. If time allows and students express an interest, you may wish to discuss in detail when and how to use formal and informal language in cards.

4. If students do not already have e-mail accounts, there are many websites where free accounts can be obtained, such as http://www.hotmail.com, http://www.yahoo.com, and so on.

**Student's name:** _____**Date:**_____

**PART I. Write five "thank-you" card expressions.**

1. _____ 2. _____

3. _____ 4. _____

5. _____

**PART II. Write a "thank-you" card for each occasion.**

1. Your friend's brother helped you move into a new apartment.

3. Your neighbor invited you to eat dinner and you had a nice evening.

2. Your friend gave you a very nice gift for your birthday.

4. Your teacher brought you flowers when you were sick.

**Activity 4.1**

**Further Activities:**

1. Have students review a number of holidays and attempt to match e-cards to them. They should search for common expressions that relate to a particular holiday.

2. Visit a greeting card store and browse as a class (ESL only).

**Modify the Level:**

1. Intermediate students can compose a handwritten "thank-you" note.

2. Intermediate students can make a list of occasions (i.e., weddings, funerals, graduations, etc.), and practice the expressions people use with one another at these times.

3. Advanced students may compose a formal "thank-you" letter to a person or organization that was helpful to them.

# Circumnavigation
### *Corresponding With Key Pals*

| | |
|---|---|
| **Integrated Skills:** | WRITING; Reading; Culture |
| **Level:** | Beginning |

**Objectives:**

- Students will read about and select potential key pals.

*HOTS* Students will create a key pal profile and send it to prospective correspondents.

*HOTS* Students will edit one another's work.

*HOTS* Students will communicate meaningfully in the target language.

**Website Address(es):**

http://www.mightymedia.com/keypals —*Key pal link*

http://www.epals.com —*Key pal link*
➔Under "Connect", click "Find E-pals" ➔Choose and click on a country➔Look for profiles of key pals

*Click the "Search" button on your browser or use any search engine*
➔Find any one of a number of sites for key pal projects and register your students

**Suggested Time:** Two 50-minute sessions

**Computing Skills:** E-mailing

**Additional Resources:** E-mail accounts for students

# TEACHER GUIDE

| | |
|---|---|
| **Preactivity Day 1**  | **Schema Building:**<br>1. Introduce the activity by asking students if they write letters to their friends, and if they are familiar with the concept of a *pen pal*.<br><br>2. Introduce them to the idea of *key pals*, and e-mail exchanges. Ask students about their concepts of e-mail exchanges, e-mail etiquette, their personal experiences, and so on. |

| | | |
|---|---|---|
| **Activity Days 1–2**  | **Grouping:**<br>Individual | **Setup:**<br>Students will select potential key pals, write profiles for themselves, and engage in an e-mail exchange in the target language. |
| | 1. Distribute worksheets, and have students visit an exchange center. Here they read the profiles of potential e-mail key pals. Ask them to choose three or four potential people, and list them on Part I of their worksheets.<br><br>2. Have students make a list of basic, personal data on Part II of the worksheet, from which they create a simple introductory letter for themselves.<br><br>3. Have students exchange introduction letters with their classmates, who then correct as many mistakes as they can find.<br><br>4. Ask students to send their corrected letter to their prospective key pals (and one copy to you). | |

| | |
|---|---|
| **Postactivity Day 2**  | Students begin an e-mail exchange with their new partner(s) and keep a portfolio of their e-mails and replies (printouts). Periodically check the progress of the portfolio. (Encourage students to seek out new key pals if the ones they have chosen do not respond). |

**Tips:**
1. If students do not already have e-mail accounts, there are many websites where free accounts can be obtained, such as http://www.hotmail.com, http://www.yahoo.com, and so on.

2. For practice, you may wish to initially have students participate in an e-mail exchange with a classmate they do not know well.

3. Offer students e-mail safety tips (i.e., to guard their passwords closely, to not give out personal information, such as address and telephone number, to a stranger, etc.).

**Student's name:** _____Date:_____

## WORKSHEET

**PART I.**   **Choose three or four people from the sites with whom you want to make friends.**

*Partner 1*

Name: _____

E-mail: _____

Nationality: _____

*Interesting Points: _____

_____

_____

*Partner 3*

Name: _____

E-mail: _____

Nationality: _____

*Interesting Points: _____

_____

_____

*Partner 2*

Name: _____

E-mail: _____

Nationality: _____

*Interesting Points: _____

_____

_____

*Partner 4*

Name: _____

E-mail: _____

Nationality: _____

*Interesting Points: _____

_____

_____

*hobby, sign of the zodiac, blood type, favorite food, celebrity, singer, etc.*

**PART II.**   **Now it's your turn.**

Name: _____

E-mail: _____

Nationality: _____

*Interesting Points: _____

_____

**Activity 4.2**

**Further Activities:**

1. The class may build its own key pal list and post it on the Internet.

2. Students can orally present their key pals to their classmates.

3. Students can communicate with their e-mail partners in a chat room.

4. As need arises, students can share with the class various expressions and/or emoticons in their e-mails that they do not understand, and learn from them.

**Modify the Level:**

1. Intermediate students can assume an identity and acquire an anonymous e-mail address (e.g., "456@anymail.com"). They can then e-mail their classmates, and through questions and answers, attempt to guess one another's identities.

2. Advanced students can subscribe to a listserv (e-mail mailing list, usually topically oriented) that interests them and participate, at least once, in a discussion. Have students report what happened to the class.

# Starfish
## *Compiling a Celebrity Biography*

| | |
|---|---|
| **Integrated Skills:** | WRITING; Reading |

| | |
|---|---|
| **Level:** | Intermediate |

**Objectives:**

- Students will extract information about a famous person from an Internet search.

*HOTS* Students will compose an autobiographical-style paragraph, assuming the identity of the celebrity they chose to research.

*HOTS* Students will generate relevant questions or comments about other students' paragraphs.

*HOTS* Students will revise their paragraphs by incorporating the feedback they received from others.

**Website Address(es):** *Click the "Search" button on your browser or use any search engine*

**Suggested Time:** Three 50-minute sessions

**Computing Skills:**
- Performing a search
- Word processing

**Additional Resources:** Diskette (optional)

# TEACHER GUIDE

| | |
|---|---|
| **Preactivity**<br>**Day 1**<br> | **Schema Building:**<br>1. Introduce the activity by asking students what famous person they like or admire the most. Prompt them if necessary, offering examples of famous scientists, authors, political leaders, actors, musicians, athletes, and so on.<br>2. Ask students to write autobiographical paragraphs, providing information about themselves, such as their interests and personal accomplishments.<br>3. Discuss the paragraphs, emphasizing the different styles and ways to write an introductory paragraph. Have students look at the model paragraph provided on page 110. |

| | | |
|---|---|---|
| **Activity**<br>**Day 2**<br>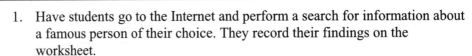 | **Grouping:**<br>Individual | **Setup:**<br>Each student will choose a famous person, about whom they will gather biographical information. Students will then assume the identity of that person, and compose an autobiographical-style paragraph in the first person. |

| | |
|---|---|
| | 1. Have students go to the Internet and perform a search for information about a famous person of their choice. They record their findings on the worksheet.<br><br>2. Assuming the identities of the people they researched, students write an autobiographical-style paragraph or paragraphs using a word processing program. Be certain that students save their work to diskettes or to the hard drives of their computers, and allow their documents to remain visible on their screens.<br><br>3. Students visit at least three computer stations used by other classmates. They read their classmates' work, and, on the same screen, type at least one question asking for additional information or clarification about the personality represented in the paragraph.<br><br>4. When everyone has finished, have students print their paragraphs and the questions asked by their peers. |

| | |
|---|---|
| **Postactivity**<br>**Day 3**<br> | 1. Ask students to consider the questions offered by their classmates. They return to the Internet and search to find answers to as many of their classmates' questions as possible.<br><br>2. Have students rewrite their paragraphs, incorporating their revisions. They print the new paragraph and submit it, along with the first draft, for assessment. |

**Tips:**

1. Emphasize very strongly that students are absolutely forbidden to copy information verbatim from their readings (plagiarism). All content must be in the students' own words. (A few appropriate and well-cited references may be acceptable).

2. You may wish to allow students to make use of the spelling and grammar checking functions in the word processing program. If you do not choose to allow it, encourage students to correct their peers.

3. Some students may be asked more questions than others. Circulate and verify that each student has a sufficient number of questions to answer.

**Student's name:** _____**Date:**_____

## WORKSHEET

1.  What is the name of a famous person that you very much admire and respect?

    _____

2.  Why do you admire or respect this person?

    _____

    _____

3.  What is (was) this person's profession?

    _____

4.  List the person's basic biographical information (age, gender, nationality, etc.).

    _____

    _____

5.  List the person's most important accomplishments.

    _____

    _____

    _____

    _____

6.  Find one or several little-known facts about the person.

    _____

    _____

    _____

    _____

Activity 4.3

## Further Activities:

1. After reading one another's paragraphs, students form pairs and role play interviewers and celebrities.

2. Students compose their paragraphs, concealing the names of the famous people in question. Their classmates read the paragraphs, and attempt to determine the identity of the celebrities through deduction, and perhaps by additional research on the Internet.

## Modify the Level:

1. Beginning students can compose short self-introductory paragraphs.

2. Advanced students can exchange paragraphs and expand the work of their peers into short biographies, providing details on the person's accomplishments (written in the third person).

3. Advanced students can research two famous people, and compare and contrast their accomplishments in an essay.

## MODEL PARAGRAPH:

My name is Ted Koppel. I am an anchorman for the television news show called *Nightline*. Have you seen the show? People say that I have a wide knowledge of political issues. In my show, I hope to convey the issues as objectively as possible. I also want to make them as clear as possible. In order to do this, I have to ask difficult questions of the people I interview, and sometimes this makes me seem arrogant. I try not to judge people, and I have no political agenda. I just want to give people a balanced view of the issues.

**Activity 4.4 - Intermediate**

# A Place in the Sun
### *Applying to Colleges*

| | |
|---|---|
| **Integrated Skills:** | WRITING; Reading; Culture |
| **Level:** | Intermediate |

**Objectives:**

*HOTS*    Students will compare universities and select one according to their needs.

*HOTS*    Students will compose an application essay.

*HOTS*    Students will edit one another's work.

*HOTS*    Students will communicate with a university to obtain information.

**Website Address(es):**

*Note: The first segments of the URLs lead to the main page of the institutio—type in the additional part of the address for the applications.*

http://usfweb.usf.edu/enroll/admiss/application.html
—*University of South Florida*
➔Choose "USF Undergraduate Application"

http://hardy.success.gatech.edu/apply/fresh2.html
—*Georgia Tech*
➔Choose the printable version

http://www.hcc.cc.fl.us/services/admissions/admissions.asp
—*Hillsborough Community College*
➔Choose "Hillsborough Community College Application For Admission"

http://www.duke.edu/web/ug-admissions —*Duke University*
➔Click "Applying to Duke" ➔Click "The Application for Admission in 2***"

**Suggested Time:**    Three 50-minute sessions

**Hardware Requirements:**    Printer

**Software Requirements:**
- Adobe® Acrobat® Reader

  *A copy should be installed on all computers to be used prior to the lesson. A free copy is available from www.adobe.com/products/acrobat/*

- Word processing program

**Computing Skills:**
- Downloading
- Performing a search

**Additional Resources:**    Diskette (optional)

# TEACHER GUIDE

| | |
|---|---|
| **Preactivity**<br>**Day 1**<br> | **Schema Building:**<br>1. Introduce the activity by having students imagine that they have each won a scholarship to study at a university in the United States. Have students describe how they would select a university. What criteria would be instrumental in their decisions?<br><br>2. Have students brainstorm on what they know about application procedures and forms, as well as information required of them by a university. |

| | | |
|---|---|---|
| **Activity**<br>**Days 1–2**<br> | **Grouping:**<br>Individual | **Setup:**<br>Students will practice applying to a university of their choice. |
| | 1. Students access university websites and search for programs, activities, departments, and degrees that interest them, and complete their worksheets.<br><br>2. Have students locate application forms for the schools, print them out, and complete them.<br><br>3. Using their worksheets as guides, students write application essays. Have them print and save their work, and exchange their essays for their peers to edit.<br><br>4. Students revise their work, and then print the final drafts of their essays to turn in with their applications (see Tip 2). | |

| | |
|---|---|
| **Postactivity**<br>**Day 3**<br> | Have students compose letters to the universities of their choice requesting a catalogue and a schedule of classes, as well as information on financial aid, housing, special requirements of international students, and specific university programs. Students e-mail the final drafts of their letters to the universities (and send a copy to you). |

 **Tips:**

1. Some universities have online registration, while others expect students to download and print out the applications. In either case, applications should be printed so students may practice filling them out correctly. In the latter case, it may be necessary to download additional software to be able to read and print the file (such as Adobe® Acrobat® Reader).

2. Save either to a diskette or to a hard drive.

3. To make the comparison of different universities easier, students can open new windows for each university and toggle back and forth between them.

4. If time is a concern, you may wish to assign part of the essay writing as homework.

**Student's name:** _____ **Date:** _____

## WORKSHEET

### PART I.

1. What is your area of interest (topic of study)?

_____

2. What interests you about this field?

_____

_____

_____

3. What are your career goals?

_____

_____

_____

### PART II.

1. Which university interests you the most? _____

2. What features of the university do you find attractive?

   A. _____

   B. _____

   C. _____

   D. _____

3. Which program appeals you at this university?

_____

4. What aspects of this program interest you the most?

   A. _____

   B. _____

   C. _____

   D. _____

5. Why do you think you would be a good addition to the university's program? What are your strengths (accomplishments, experience, etc.)?

   A. _____

   B. _____

   C. _____

   D. _____

## Activity 4.4

### Further Activities:

1. Have students play the roles of university admissions officers and write reply letters to one another's applications.

2. In small groups students explain to each other exactly why they chose the universities they did. Have them take finances into consideration.

### Modify the Level:

1. Beginning students can complete printed university application forms.

2. Advanced students can search for scholarship information and apply for one, making a convincing case for themselves.

# Rising Tides

*Reporting on Global Warming*

| | |
|---|---|
| **Integrated Skills:** | WRITING; Reading; Speaking; Culture |
| **Level:** | Advanced |

**Objectives:**

- Students will identify an environmental issue related to global warming.

*HOTS* Students will collect relevant information and synthesize this into a newspaper-style article.

*HOTS* Students will discuss their findings and collaborate to refine their written work.

**Website Address(es):**

http://www.epa.gov/globalwarming/ —*Global warming information*

➔For Part I of the worksheet, click on "Climate," read the information ➔Next, click on the "Impacts" link, read and exit ➔Then click on the "Actions" link, read and exit

➔For Part II of the worksheet, click on "In the News"➔Click on "Speeches"

**Suggested Time:** Four to five 50-minute sessions

**Hardware Requirements:** Printer

**Software Requirements:** Word processing program

**Additional Resources:** Diskette (optional)

# TEACHER GUIDE

| | |
|---|---|
| **Preactivity Day 1**  | **Schema Building:**<br><br>1. Introduce the activity by showing pictures, articles, and/or video concerning an environmental issue.<br><br>2. Ask students what they know about environmental issues. Have them brainstorm to create a list of environmental concerns (global warming, air pollution, water depletion, etc.).<br><br>3. Ask students how environmental concerns are addressed in their country(-ies). |

| | | |
|---|---|---|
| **Activity Days 2–3**  | **Grouping:**<br>Individual | **Setup:**<br>Students will collect relevant information concerning global warming, and compose newspaper-style articles. |

1. Distribute worksheets and have students go to the provided website. Have students gather general information on the global warming issue and complete Part I of their worksheets.

2. Have students identify one aspect of the global warming problem that interests them, and read *several* of the speeches at the provided website. Students read in depth about that aspect, and take notes on Part II of the worksheets.

3. Using the worksheet as a guide, each student composes a two-page paper in a word processing program. The paper should be in the style of a newspaper article and contain an introduction, a brief summary of the problem, an in-depth development of one aspect of the global warming issue, and a conclusion. Be certain students cite their sources.

4. Have students save their papers to diskettes or to their hard drives, and print them.

| | |
|---|---|
| **Postactivity Days 4–5**  | 1. Students exchange papers and conduct a peer-review session.<br><br>2. Ask students to retrieve their papers, make revisions, and print.<br><br>3. Hold a class discussion of the issue, allowing students the opportunity to present their points of view and their findings.<br><br>4. If necessary, allow students to make additional revisions to their papers. They print a final draft and submit all three copies to you for review/assessment. |

 **Tips:**

1. Students' articles may be submitted to the school newspaper, or students may compose a "Global Warming" journal of their own.

2. Both the composition and revisions of the paper can be done at home to save time.

3. You may wish to assess only the final draft of the paper, or you may want to look at all three copies in order to evaluate progress.

**Student's name:** _____**Date:**_____

## WORKSHEET

**PART I.** **You are a newspaper reporter, and you wish to write an article about a particular aspect of the global warming issue. Find out what you can about global warming (use additional paper as necessary to write your answers).**

1. What is global warming?

_____

2. What do we know? What are the causes?

_____

_____

3. How serious is the problem now? How serious will it be in the future?

_____

_____

4. What is being done?

_____

_____

5. What can I do?

_____

_____

**PART II.** **Identify one aspect of the global warming problem that interests you. Read and take notes on several speeches that deal with that aspect.**

My interest is:

_____

Notes:

_____

_____

_____

_____

_____

_____

_____

**Activity 4.5**

**Further Activities:**

1. Have students research local environmental concerns and put together a newsletter or presentation to be distributed to other students at their school.

2. Contact a local environmental organization or agency and volunteer as a class.

3. Have students write to or e-mail local governmental representatives about an environmental concern.

**Modify the Level:**

1. Beginning students can examine one section of the website. Choose an appropriate section and create a worksheet with multiple-choice and fill-in-the-blank questions. You may also wish to extract certain useful phrases from the text and explain them in detail.

2. Intermediate students can also complete the worksheet by gathering information from the website. Instruct students to put the answers in their own words.

3. Intermediate students can refer to the website and compile a list of tips on things students can do to save the environment (this would replace Part II of the worksheet).

# Exploring the Seven Seas
## *Creating a Collaborative Travelogue*

| | |
|---|---|
| **Integrated Skills:** | WRITING; Reading; Speaking |
| **Level:** | Advanced |

**Objectives:**

*HOTS* Students will collaborate to select and extract pictures from an existing travelogue.

*HOTS* Students will generate ideas for a fictional journey.

*HOTS* Students will compose a travel narrative.

*HOTS* Students will compare narratives and match them to the appropriate photos.

 **Website address(es):** http://www.nationalgeographic.com/photography/archive/index.html
—*Photo and travelogue site*
➔Click on any travelogue of interest

 **Suggested Time:** Three to four 50-minute sessions

**Hardware Requirements:** Printer

**Software Requirements:**
- Word processing program
- Presentation program (optional)

**Computing Skills:**
- Inserting photos/graphics
- Downloading

 **Additional Resources:** Diskette (optional)

| | |
|---|---|
| **Preactivity**<br>**Day 1**<br> | **Schema Building:**<br>1. Ask students how they remember their travel experiences (keep journals, take photos, buy souvenirs, etc.).<br><br>2. Ask students what kinds of places they might visit if they wanted an adventurous vacation.<br><br>3. Introduce the idea of a *travelogue.*<br><br>**Modeling:**<br>1. Guide students through any one of the travelogues at the provided website. Have students brainstorm how the photos support the narrative. Call attention to the characteristics of a travelogue (dates, sequence, style, audience, etc.)<br><br>2. As a class, choose three pictures and brainstorm together a short, logical, and sequential narrative.<br><br>3. Deconstruct the students' narrative and model the composition of an outline. |

| | | |
|---|---|---|
| **Activity**<br>**Days 2–3**<br> | **Grouping:**<br>Small groups | **Setup:**<br>Students will create fictional narratives in the form of journals or travelogues to accompany a series of selected pictures. |

| | |
|---|---|
| | 1. Assign students to small groups and distribute the worksheets.<br><br>2. Redirect groups to the National Geographic (or other) site and ask them to discuss and agree on a selection of three photos to depict a fictional journey of their own. (The photos do not necessarily have to be sequential or come from the same travelogue).<br><br>3. Once they have made their selections, ask each group to complete the worksheet, describing their photos as thoroughly as possible.<br><br>4. Have the groups download the photos they've selected to a diskette or to the hard drives of their computers.<br><br>5. Each group inserts its photos into a word processing or presentation program document. Under each photo have students write an original, fictional, 100-word narrative of a trip. Stories should be logical and sequential. Have students print the final draft and turn it in for assessment. |

| | |
|---|---|
| **Postactivity**<br>**Day 4**<br> | Have students print out their texts and photos on separate sheets (as many copies as there are groups in the class, themselves excepted). Shuffle the piles of photos and texts and distribute to each group. The groups then read and try to match the narratives to the photos. |

 **Tips:**
1. Emphasize that students are to create *original* narratives in their travelogues.
2. If downloading the pictures is difficult, they may be printed and pasted into the text.
3. Be aware that picture files can be extremely large and cause delays in processing time.
4. Be certain students are aware that publication, distribution, or reproduction of copyrighted material must be restricted to classroom use to comply with fair-use regulations.
5. Note that this lesson may be appropriate either prior to or after a class field trip.

**Students' names:** _____ **Date:** _____

## WORKSHEET

**PART I. Answer the following questions after you have chosen your photos and discussed your imaginary voyage.**

1. When did your trip occur? _____

2. Where did you go?

_____

_____

3. Whom did you go with? _____

4. What did you do there?

_____

_____

_____

_____

5. Why did you go? _____

_____

6. What will be the title of your narrative? _____

7. Where did you locate the photos you will use?   **http://** _____

**http://** _____   **http://** _____

**PART II. Here are some tips to help you write.**

- Begin your narrative with an attention-getting statement. Say something that will intrigue your reader and make them want to know more.

- Give many supporting details in your narrative to give your reader a clear picture of what happened during your travels.

- Use many adjectives. Be certain to include transitions between sentences as well as between the ideas and events expressed in your narrative.

- Try to make your narrative dramatic, funny, or ironic.

- End your story in a surprising or amusing way.

**Activity 4.6**

## Further Activities:

1. Have students each bring in three of their own photos and use them to compose an original travelogue.

2. Have students go on a photo shooting trip of local places and things of interest and compose real travelogues of their visits.

3. Pass out one photo per student, and have the class compose an impromptu oral travel narrative. Go around the room and have each student in turn continue the narrative, trying to make a logical transition from the previous student's portion of the story to one that corresponds to their own photo.

4. Ask students to bring some of their own photos to class. They then randomly swap pictures with their classmates. Students hold up the pictures they wound up with and give an impromptu, imaginary oral travelogue.

## Modify the Level:

1. Beginning students can write a single sentence per photo.

2. Intermediate students can use the beginning section of an authentic photo caption and continue the description in their own words.

# Surfing the Planet:
# Exploring Culture

# A Rationale & Guide for Integrating Culture into English Language Instruction

## Jeffra Flaitz

How hard can it be to teach culture? Doesn't it simply consist of pointing out relevant sites on a map, identifying typical foods, listening to samples of the target culture's musical traditions, viewing the works of its most prominent artists, determining what religions are represented there, and examining the structure of its government? Aren't fiestas, field trips, guest lectures, bulletin boards, pen pals, and craft projects part of teaching culture, too? This doesn't seem hard. In fact, it seems fun. And it is. But activities of this kind represent only the tip of the iceberg, so to speak. They reflect what is external and explicit. But the real essence, and the real danger, of an iceberg is not the 30 percent floating at the surface, but the remaining 70 percent down below. Above the surface of the "ocean of culture," we find *artifacts*—laws and schools, food and clothing, sports and politics, words and ceremonies. Below the surface are values, attitudes, philosophies, beliefs, assumptions, taboos, and judgements. Freud's now-familiar use of the terms "conscious" and "subconscious" may help us to understand this concept, and Nelson Brooks, one of the pioneers in the teaching of foreign-language culture, referred to the distinction as one of "surface culture" versus "deep culture."

Understandably enough, foreign language teachers and materials developers typically explore only a portion of the topic of culture, the tip of the iceberg. Why? No doubt because that is what is visible and, thus, more readily teachable—a case of the means justifying the ends. Surely citizens of the new millenium will not be satisfied with such a limited approach to the development of cross-cultural understanding. We teach culture in our foreign language classrooms because we believe our students not only need to know *what* other people do, but *why* they do it. Edward T. Hall extended this goal in 1959 in his book *The Silent Language*. He wrote, "Our real job is not to understand foreign culture, but to understand our own."[*] Thus, the exploration of deep culture leads to a much more insightful sense of self, the foundation for understanding others.

Admittedly, the task is daunting. How can we teach deep culture when it is all but hidden? The solution is to carefully plan the study of culture. Establish goals. Balance study of surface culture artifacts with attention to deep culture foundations. Do not diminish the importance of culture study by relegating it to a Friday afternoon slot. Help students to understand the purpose of culture study. Most importantly, focus on process. The study of culture is one of evolution and discovery. Teachers often grow along with their students if this approach is taken, and may then serve as models for lifelong culture learning. Culture is the focus of the lessons in this chapter, which, of course, include additional skills.

---

[*]Hall, Edward T. (1959). *The silent language*. Greenwich, CT: Fawcett, p.30

# TEACHING TIPS FOR CULTURE

**Modeling:**

♦ Demonstrate your own appreciation for the values of the target culture, even if they may conflict with your own.

♦ Avoid using stereotypes.

**Preparation:**

♦ Establish at the outset of the course the specific goals you have for the teaching of culture.

♦ Plan extended culture units rather than treating culture topics piecemeal.

♦ Explore the expanding variety of resources offered by the Internet.

♦ Plan to test students' culture knowledge.

♦ Use as many concrete examples as you can to supplement your lessons.

♦ Discuss, evaluate, and expand students' background knowledge prior to delving deeply into any culture topic.

♦ Focus on cross-cultural similarities as well as differences.

♦ Identify cultural universals.

**Negotiation:**

♦ Choose culture topics that lend themselves to students' inquiry.
  Solicit topics for culture study from your students.

♦ Adopt a compare/contrast approach to enable students to take a positive, yet critical, look at themselves and others.

♦ Use your students as resources for information, perception, and interpretation of the values and behaviors of both their home and the target cultures.

**Expectations:**

♦ Allow students to explore and grow at their own pace; cultural awareness and sensitivity cannot be forced.

♦ Focus on cross-cultural understanding.

♦ Empower your students with the responsibility to learn about themselves as products of a culture.

**Motivation:**

♦ Encourage students' curiosity. Urge them to ask questions and find answers.

♦ Give students the opportunity to "become" a member of the target culture through carefully chosen activities.

♦ Offer students real interaction with the target culture via e-mail and other technology-based mechanisms.

**Level:**

♦ Introduce deep culture study at the middle school level, and continue to infuse greater amounts as students progress through grade levels.

♦ To the extent possible, use the target language to teach about the target culture.

# CULTURE TIPS FOR STUDENTS

♦ Ask "why?" People from other cultures might have logical explanations for why they do something differently.

♦ Ask yourself why you believe what you do. Remember that you are influenced by your own culture.

♦ Actively look for ways to learn more about the target language culture.

♦ Identify what interests you most in your own culture, and look for information on the same topic in the target culture.

♦ Try not to be judgmental. Keep an open mind.

♦ Try to imagine yourself as a member of the target culture. What kinds of things would you do? How would you solve problems? How might you think in certain situations?

♦ Enjoy the journey. Culture study brings deeper insight andunderstanding.

# Stars on the Water
## *Interpreting Horoscopes*

| | |
|---|---|
| **Integrated Skills:** | CULTURE; Reading; Speaking |
| **Level:** | Beginning |
| **Objectives:** | ■ Students will identify and extract key adjectives and verbs from horoscopes. |
| | ■ Students will discover and discuss the characteristics of their astrological signs. |
| | *HOTS* Students will interpret images related to superstitions. |
| | *HOTS* Students will compare and contrast prediction-related beliefs in the target language and in their own culture(s). |
| **Website Address(es):** | http://astrology.yahoo.com/ —*Site for horoscopes* |
| **Suggested Time:** | Three 50-minute sessions |
| **Computing Skills:** | Performing a search |
| **Additional Resources:** | Newspaper or magazine with horoscopes |

# TEACHER GUIDE

| Preactivity Day 1  | **Schema Building:** |
|---|---|
| | 1. Introduce the notion of astrology and horoscopes by showing students the symbols of the zodiac. What do students already know? |
| | 2. Ask students for their birthdays (review days and months), and determine what signs they are. |
| | 3. Show students copies of their horoscopes (i.e., from a newspaper or magazine). |
| | 4. If time allows, ask students to form pairs. They should list the astrological signs of their families and friends, and share the list with their partners. |
| | 5. Ask students for their opinions of this type of fortune telling. Do they believe there is any truth to it, or do they think it is superstition? *(Be sure students understand this word)*. Ask students if they have other ways of predicting the future in their countries. |

| Activity Day 2  | **Grouping:** Individual | **Setup:** Students will access their horoscopes and extract vocabulary that describes people who share their astrological signs. |
|---|---|---|
| | 1. Distribute worksheets, and have students go to the horoscope website. Once there, they should click on their astrological sign. | |
| | 2. Have students extract just the main ideas, words, and phrases from the horoscope. Have students complete Part I of the worksheet. | |
| | 3. Group students by astrological sign and ask them to share what they found. (If there are students without partners, group them together). They should come to an agreement and present their signs to the rest of the class (i.e., "Virgos are neat and organized . . ."). | |

| Post activity Day 3  | 1. Regroup the students into evenly sized small groups. Ask them to complete Part II of the worksheet (see Tip 4 for the answers to item 1). |
|---|---|
| | 2. Have the groups report to the rest of the class. |

**Tips:**

1. As part of the preactivity, provide a glossary of keywords for understanding the descriptions of horoscopes.

2. You may wish to distribute simplified versions of the horoscopes.

3. Take into account the composition of students in the class and be aware that some students may find other students' definitions of "superstitions" offensive.

4. On the worksheet, the symbols in Part II represent, from left to right, bad luck (cat), good luck (horseshoe), and bad luck (number 13).

Student's name: _____ Date:_____

# WORKSHEET

## PART I.   Your Horoscope

Your date of birth: _____

Your astrological sign: _____

Read your horoscope and answer below:

1.   According to your horoscope, you are (adjective):

   *Example:*   *friendly*

   a. _____

   b. _____

   c. _____

2.   According to your horoscope, you (verb):

   *Example:*   *like to argue*

   a. _____

   b. _____

   c. _____

## PART II.   Discussing Beliefs

1. Here are three belief symbols from Western, European culture. Can you guess what they mean?

_____   _____   _____

2. Are they similar to or different from beliefs in your country?

_____   _____   _____

3. Draw a symbol of a belief from your country. Explain it to your group.

# Activity 5.1

**Further Activities:**

1. Have students look again at the website and repeat the activity with the Chinese horoscope. Schema building should include the animals in the Chinese zodiac. Have students compare and contrast their Chinese horoscopes and their zodiac signs.

2. In groups, have students choose a person (real or imaginary) and compose a simple horoscope for that person.

**Modify the Level:**

1. Intermediate/advanced students can compose "fortune cookie" fortunes for one another (e.g., "A bright future awaits you"). Students can draw fortunes at random.

2. Advanced students can share unique superstitions that exist in their cultures, and discussions can follow regarding superstitions as a whole.

# The Roaring Surf
*Exploring Animal Sounds*

| | |
|---|---|
| **Integrated Skills:** | CULTURE; Reading; Speaking |

---

| | |
|---|---|
| **Level:** | Beginning |

---

**Objectives:**

- Students describe the physical characteristics of animals.

 *HOTS* Students will make cross-linguistic comparisons of onomatopoeic representations of animal sounds.

*HOTS* Students will infer the relationship between onomatopoeic sounds and their written representations.

---

 **Website Address(es):** http://www.georgetown.edu/cball/animals/animals.html
—*Animal sounds*

Note: You may wish to download in advance the animal sounds you will use for Part II of the lesson.

http://members.tripod.com/Thryomanes/MammalSounds.html#cats
—*Cat sounds* (URL is case sensitive)

http://members.tripod.com/Thryomanes/MammalSounds.html#dogs
—*Dog sounds* (URL is case sensitive)

---

 **Suggested Time:** Two 50-minute sessions

---

 **Computing Skills:** Downloading

---

**Software Requirements:** Real™Audio®

*To save time, prior to beginning the lesson, download and install Real™Audio® onto the hard drives of all the computers to be used.*

# TEACHER GUIDE

| Preactivity Day 1  | **Schema Building:** Show students pictures of many different kinds of animals. Ask them to describe the animals in as many ways as they can think of. **Modeling:** 1. From a website, CD, cassette, or other source, play to the students the sound of a rooster crowing. Students should record on paper how people in their home countries write the sound the rooster makes (i.e., *cocorico*, *kokehkoko*, etc.) If students are all from the same culture, have them try to guess what the English equivalent might be instead. 2. Have students form pairs. Ask students to compare their answers. (If your students are all from the same linguistic background, move on to the activity). |
|---|---|

| Activity Day 1  | **Grouping:** Pairs | **Setup:** Students will compare, discuss, and research animal sounds as perceived by English speakers. |
|---|---|---|

| | 1. Have students go to one of the provided Internet sites and click on the name of each animal listed on their worksheet. Ask them to complete Part I of the worksheet. 2. To raise awareness among students that some words are written in a way that represents a sound (*onomatopoeia*), play three sounds cats make and three sounds made by dogs. Have students look at Part II of the worksheet and ask them to guess which words correspond to the sounds you played for them. Have them explain their answers before playing and discussing the other choices. |
|---|---|

| Postactivity Day 2  | 1. Students return to the Internet, and choose three animals whose sounds are represented differently in several languages. Have them share what they found with the rest of the class. 2. Have students make and compile two decks of cards. One deck contains the names of animals, and the other contains the English representations of the sounds the animals make. Students shuffle the decks, turn cards face down to hide the content, and play a memory game, attempting to match the animals to their sounds. |
|---|---|

**Tips:**

1. Be sure to locate and download and/or record the sound of the rooster crowing prior to the class.

2. For Part II of the worksheet, use the provided website and download (and/or record) the sounds you will use prior to the class.

Students' names: _____ Date:_____

## WORKSHEET

### PART I.   Animal Sounds

**How are these animals' sounds written in English and in your language?**

|  | ENGLISH | YOUR LANGUAGE _____ |
|---|---|---|
| **ANIMAL** | | |
| 1. **Cow** | _____ | _____ |
| 2. **Dog** | _____ | _____ |
| 3. **Chick** | _____ | _____ |
| 4. **Cat** | _____ | _____ |
| 5. **Frog** | _____ | _____ |
| 6. **Duck** | _____ | _____ |
| 7. **Pig** | _____ | _____ |
| 8. **Sheep** | _____ | _____ |

### PART II.   More animal sounds

**You will hear several sounds. Place a number (1, 2, or 3) by the word you think best describes the sound you hear.**

**1.**

Howl

Hiss     Meow

**2.**

Growl

Bark     Yelp

**Activity 5.2**

**Further Activities:**

1. Discuss other onomatopoeic words related to pain, laughing, crying, loud noises, and so on.

2. Students may search through comic books for additional onomatopoeic words.

**Modify the Level:**

1. Intermediate/advanced students can search the Internet for less common pets.

2. Intermediate/advanced students can discuss and compile a list of reasons why people choose certain animals as pets.

3. Advanced students can do a detailed search for the range of services dedicated to pet owners (pet psychiatry, pet stores, pet schools, pet cemeteries, etc.)

# Clambake!
## *Relating Food & Culture*

| | |
|---|---|
| **Integrated Skills:** | CULTURE; Reading; Speaking |

---

| | |
|---|---|
| **Level:** | Intermediate |

---

**Objectives:**

- Students will interpret the cultural relevance of a traditional/typical dish.

- Students will identify and describe the characteristics of this dish.

 *HOTS* Students will recognize and discuss the relationship between food and tradition.

---

 **Website Address(es):**

http://soar.berkeley.edu/recipes/ethnic/austalian/
—*Australian recipes*

http://soar.berkeley.edu/recipes/ethnic/british/
—*British recipes*

http://soar.berkeley.edu/recipes/ethnic/irish/
—*Irish recipes*

http://soar.berkeley.edu/recipes/ethnic/canadian/
—*Canadian recipes*

http://soar.berkeley.edu/recipes/ethnic/cajun/
—*Cajun recipes*

http://soar.berkeley.edu/recipes/ethnic/native/
—*Native American recipes*

---

 **Suggested Time:** | Three 50-minute sessions

---

**Computing Skills:** | Performing a search

# TEACHER GUIDE

| | |
|---|---|
| **Preactivity Day 1**  | **Schema Building:** <br><br> 1. Introduce the activity by asking students to talk about the kinds of foods they see as very traditional or typical to their homeland(s). Discuss when and why these foods are eaten. <br><br> 2. Have students brainstorm about any traditional foods they know of in English-speaking countries. <br><br> 3. Introduce new vocabulary, such as *dish, recipe,* cooking measurements, and words relating to styles. <br><br> **Modeling:** <br> Present a dish from an English-speaking country to the students by preparing it for them to taste, explaining its role in the culture, and distributing copies of the recipe. |
| **Activity Day 2**  | **Grouping:** Individual     **Setup:** Students will search for a traditional food associated with an English-speaking country and present what they have found to the class. <br><br> 1. Distribute worksheets, and have students go to one of the provided websites and search for a traditional dish eaten in an English-speaking country. <br><br> 2. Have students read for information and complete the worksheet. <br><br> 3. If time allows, have students begin their preparations for the postactivity. Unfinished work may be completed as homework. |
| **Postactivity Day 3**  | Have students prepare a presentation (consider using presentation software or poster boards) about the food they researched (additional research may be necessary). They will need pictures of the dish as well as a copy of the recipe for their classmates. |

 **Tips:**

1. You may wish to narrow the scope and have students concentrate on regions of a particular country.

2. For the postactivity, students may prepare the dish in question so their classmates can have a taste.

3. If students cannot find a traditional food on the Internet, you may give them suggestions, such as the ANZAC Day cookie from Australia, the Thanksgiving turkey or stuffing from the United States, haggis from Scotland, and so on.

Student's name: _____ Date:_____

# WORKSHEET

**PART I.** Look for information on a traditional or typical dish from an English-speaking country and answer the following questions.

1. What is the name of the dish? _____

2. What country and region does the dish come from? _____

3. What does the dish look like? Use several adjectives to describe the dish.

_____

_____

4. When is the dish eaten? Is there a holiday or celebration associated with the dish? What is the name of the celebration? How does this dish relate to the celebration? What is the significance of the dish?

_____

_____

_____

_____

_____

5. Who typically prepares the dish? _____

_____

**PART II.** Find a recipe for the dish you chose, and write it below.

**Activity 5.3**

**Further Activities:**

Students may bring recipes (and/or the actual dishes) from their home countries or regions to present to their classmates. Students can give a simple explanation of the significance and method of preparation of the dish to the class.

**Modify the Level:**

1. Beginning students may be assigned appropriate websites concerning specific dishes. Students can then extract and record information (such as the country, region and three important ingredients of the dish in question) onto a simplified worksheet.

2. Beginning students can explain a traditional dish from their own country to the class. They should provide visuals and other supporting information.

3. Advanced students can make a *detailed* presentation of a food and the holiday or celebration associated with it, including the process of preparation, significance, and so on.

4. Advanced students can locate, prepare, and share a dish from one of the target cultures, and explain its relevance in the culture to their classmates.

# Leprechaun Lagoon
### *Investigating Holiday Symbolism*

| | |
|---|---|
| **Integrated Skills:** | CULTURE; Reading; Writing |
| **Level:** | Intermediate |

**Objectives:**

- Students will sort and select websites about a particular holiday.

 **HOTS** Students will analyze the information and report it to the class.

**HOTS** Students will discuss the cultural symbolism of the given holiday and compare it with that of a holiday in their own culture.

**HOTS** Students will collect and organize information to create a presentation.

 **Website Address(es):**

http://wilstar.com/holidays/patrick.htm
— *St. Patrick's Day Information*

http://www.historychannel.com/stpats
— *St. Patrick's Day Information*

http://www.nando.net/toys/stpaddy/stpaddy.html
— *St. Patrick's Day Information*

 **Suggested Time:**

Three 50-minute sessions

**Computing Skills:**

- Performing a search
- E-mailing

**TEACHER GUIDE**

| | |
|---|---|
| **Preactivity Day 1**  | **Schema Building:** <br> 1. Introduce the activity by asking students to name of as many holidays celebrated in anglophone countries as they can. Add to the list where necessary. <br><br> 2. Discuss the origins of these holidays and how they are celebrated. |

| | | |
|---|---|---|
| **Activity Day 2**  | **Grouping:** <br> Individual | **Setup:** <br> Students will look for information on the Irish/American holiday of St. Patrick's Day. They will then follow the American practice of sending greeting cards, and send an e-card to a classmate. |
| | 1. Distribute worksheets, and have students go to the provided websites for information on St. Patrick's Day. Have students complete the worksheet. <br><br> 2. Have students go to an e-card site such as those provided in the St. Patrick's Day sites or at sites such as www.bluemountain.com, and send a personalized "Happy St. Patrick's Day" card to a classmate. | |

| | |
|---|---|
| **Postactivity Day 3**  | 1. As a class, have students report what they discovered about St. Patrick's Day. <br><br> 2. As a class or in groups, have the class compare this holiday with one from their own culture. Do their cultures have the equivalent of a leprechaun, a lucky plant, or a lucky color? What symbolizes good and bad luck in their cultures? <br><br> 3. In small groups, have students list and share symbols that represent holidays in their countries or regions (see Tip 2). |

**Tips:** 1. Any holiday(s) celebrated in any English-speaking country may be substituted for St. Patrick's Day.

2. EFL students can be asked to go to a greeting card website, such as www.bluemountain.com, and examine the cards available for a variety of holidays. They may wish to compare the symbols used on these cards to represent the holidays with holiday symbols in their own country, such as Jack 'o' Lanterns for Halloween (U.S.), carnations for Mother's Day (Korea), flying carp for Boy's Day (Japan), crêpes for Chandeleur's Day (France), and so on.

3. Note that students must have e-mail addresses in order to receive e-cards.

**Student's name:** _____ **Date:** _____

## WORKSHEET

### SAINT PATRICK'S DAY

1. List the addresses of Internet sites visit as you look for information.

**http://** _____ **http://** _____

**http://** _____ **http://** _____

**http://** _____ **http://** _____

2. Find the following information:

a) Who was St. Patrick? _____

_____

_____

b) Was he really Irish? _____

c) What was his most important accomplishment?

_____

_____

_____

d) What is a *shamrock*? _____

e) For what did St. Patrick use a shamrock? _____

_____

_____

f) What is the connection between St. Patrick and snakes? _____

_____

g) What will bring you good luck on St. Patrick's day? _____

_____

h) Why is the color green so important to St. Patrick's Day? _____

_____

i) Where do people celebrate St. Patrick's Day? _____

_____

j) How do people celebrate St. Patrick's Day? _____

_____

**Activity 5.4**

**Further Activities:**

1. Have students write a paper on St. Patrick's Day, comparing it to a holiday from their own culture.

2. Have students prepare a presentation (use presentation software or poster boards) on a holiday from their own culture.

3. Ask students to bring to class culturally symbolic items to explain to the rest of the class (ESL only).

4. Have students research and discuss which Anglophone holidays are similar to their own.

**Modify the Level:**

1. Beginning students can e-mail one another a St. Patrick's Day card.

2. Advanced students can play a game with traditions and customs from anglophone countries. Each student should present three traditions or customs from an English-speaking country to the class. One of the three customs will be "made up." Classmates will be challenged to determine which of the three are the real customs.

# Go With the Flow
## *Exploring Etiquette*

| **Integrated Skills:** | | CULTURE; Reading; Speaking; Writing |
|---|---|---|
| **Level:** | | Advanced |

**Objectives:**

*HOTS* — Students will distinguish appropriate from inappropriate etiquette.

▪ Students will gather information relevant to etiquette from a variety of web sites.

*HOTS* — Students will create and perform scenarios demonstrating the Do's and Don'ts of etiquette.

▪ Students will discuss and clarify their relative conception of behavioral appropriateness.

*HOTS* — Students will compare and contrast target culture etiquette to their own.

**Website Address(es):**

http://www.leaderu.com/isr/lifeinamerica/tablemanners.html
—*Table manners*

http://www.leaderu.com/isr/lifeinamerica/dosdonts.html
—*Student life etiquette*

http://www.leaderu.com/isr/lifeinamerica/dormbedroomculture.html —*Dorm room etiquette*

http://www.leaderu.com/isr/lifeinamerica/bathrooms.html
—*Bathroom etiquette*

http://www.bsu.edu/careers/manners.html
—*Table manners*

http://www.cuisinenet.com/digest/custom/etiquette/manners_intro.shtml
—*Table manners*

**Suggested Time:** Five 50-minute sessions

**Computing Skills:** Performing a search

**Additional Resources:** Props for skits (optional)

# TEACHER GUIDE

| | |
|---|---|
| **Preactivity**<br>**Day 1**<br> | **Schema Building:**<br>1. Introduce the activity by discussing with students what is meant by *etiquette*.<br><br>2. Have students brainstorm as many etiquette-related topics as they can think of (e.g., table manners, writing and responding to invitations, greetings, gift giving and receiving, tipping, bodily functions, punctuality, etc.)<br><br>3. Ask students to relate etiquette-related mistakes made by foreigners visiting their home country(ies) (see Tip 4). |

| | | |
|---|---|---|
| **Activity**<br>**Days 2–4** | **Grouping:**<br>Groups | **Setup:**<br>Students will learn about and instruct their fellow students in aspects of etiquette in the target culture. |

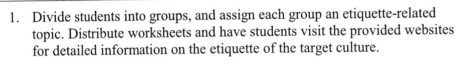

| | |
|---|---|
| **Activity**<br>**Days 2–4** | 1. Divide students into groups, and assign each group an etiquette-related topic. Distribute worksheets and have students visit the provided websites for detailed information on the etiquette of the target culture.<br><br>2. Have students compose a list of Do's and Don'ts for their topic.<br><br>3. Ask each group to compose two skits based on their Do's and Don'ts list. The first skit will exemplify proper etiquette and the second skit will represent poor manners for their topic.<br><br>4. Distribute a second set of blank worksheets to each to fill out while the other groups perform their skits.<br><br>5. Ask a group to first perform the skit on good manners, then the skit on bad manners. Class members complete the worksheet based on what they believe the group is trying to portray.<br><br>6. Hold a class discussion of what students believe was correct and incorrect in terms of good etiquette. The group in charge of the topic answers questions and corrects misconceptions. Students then revise their worksheets. |
| **Postactivity**<br>**Day 5** | Have students compose a compare and contrast paper focusing on the differences in etiquette they discovered between their own culture and the target culture. |

**Tips:**
1. Topics may include those presented in item 2 of schema building, or others as you deem appropriate.

2. Show short video clips of Do's and Don'ts from films or television programs.

3. Be certain that students research multiple aspects of their etiquette topic, such as gender differences and multiple situations (e.g., tipping should include amounts and proper methods for hotel staff, skycaps, taxi drivers, tour guides, etc., and not just restaurant servers).

4. ESL students may relate their own personal experiences and problems with etiquette in their encounters with the target culture.

**Student's name:** _____**Date:**_____

TOPIC NAME: _____

DO's

DON'Ts

_____     _____
_____     _____
_____     _____
_____     _____
_____     _____
_____     _____
_____     _____
_____     _____
_____     _____
_____     _____
_____     _____
_____     _____
_____     _____
_____     _____
_____     _____
_____     _____
_____     _____
_____     _____
_____     _____
_____     _____
_____     _____

**Activity 5.5**

**Further Activities:**

1. Have students interview native speakers to find out the reasons behind some of the target culture etiquette rules.

2. Have students interview one another about their personal experiences with etiquette *faux pas* (teach them this phrase) and relate the results to the class.

3. ESL students can visit a restaurant as a class and use appropriate etiquette. Have them discuss the appropriateness of their behavior with the restaurant staff.

**Modify the Level:**

1. Intermediate students can relate their worst etiquette experiences and ask for advice and help from their classmates.

2. Intermediate students can modify the existing activity by visiting etiquette websites you preselect. For the postactivity, students can list comparisons between the etiquette of the target culture and that of their own.

# Beach Blanket Bingo
*Critiquing Film*

| | |
|---|---|
| **Integrated Skills:** | CULTURE; Reading; Writing; Listening; Speaking |

---

**Level:** Advanced

---

**Objectives:**

♦ Students will predict the success of current movies.

*HOTS* Students will compare the criteria for popularity between films in their home countries and English-language films.

*HOTS* Students will discuss and draw conclusions about this criteria.

*HOTS* Students will create a mini-script for a film that exemplifies the features of a successful anglophone movie.

---

**Web site address(es):**

http://www.allmovie.com —*Movie summaries*
➔Look for "New in Theaters"➔Click on titles

http://www.filmland.com/boxoffice/ —*Box office reports*

http://www.joblo.com/box-office.htm —*Box office reports*

---

**Suggested Time:** Four 50-minute sessions

---

**Additional Resources:**
- Video camera (optional)
- VCR (optional)

# TEACHER GUIDE

| | |
|---|---|
| **Preactivity Day 1**  | **Schema Building:** 1. Introduce the activity by asking students what their favorite movies are. What do they like about them? 2. Next, ask students if they have ever been disappointed by a movie. What were their expectations of the film? Why did they have those expectations? 3. Finally, ask students what elements a movie must contain to be popular in their countries. |

| | | |
|---|---|---|
| **Activity Days 1–2**  | **Grouping:** Individual | **Setup:** Students will search the Internet for movie previews, predict the success of a movie in the target culture and in their own countries, and compare their predictions with current popularity ratings. |
| | 1. Distribute worksheets, and have students begin their search at the provided websites for movies currently in theaters. 2. Have students write their predictions on Part I of the worksheet. 3. Now have students go to the provided websites for box office standings and complete Part II of the worksheet. | |

| | |
|---|---|
| **Postactivity Days 3–4**  | 1. Divide students into groups and ask them to list the traits/elements of successful movies in the target culture. Have each group share their results with the class. 2. Have each group write a movie scene or a mini-script that incorporates as many of the listed traits/elements as possible (see Tip 3). 3. Have the groups act out the script, or videotape themselves in a mini-movie. |

 **Tips:**

1. As an additional preactivity, you may wish to print out movie pictures and movie titles, and have students attempt to match the title to the picture. For detailed information on given movies, go to the Internet and look for official sites from specific movie studios, such as Warner Brothers™, Touchstone℠, Paramount™, and so on.

2. If the movie has just been released, there may need to be a three-day delay between Part I and II of the worksheet.

3. Writing a movie scene or mini-script may be quite time consuming. Consider making this an out-of-class activity or a class project.

Student's name: _____ Date:_____

## WORKSHEET

**PART I.    Go to the Internet and read the descriptions of the movies.**

1. Choose the three current movies you think will be the most popular with *English speakers*, and briefly summarize the content. Next, explain your choices (actors, story line, special effects, etc.).

Movie 1: _____     Summary: _____

_____

Why do you think this movie will be popular?    _____

_____

_____

Movie 2: _____     Summary: _____

_____

Why do you think this movie will be popular?    _____

_____

Movie 3: _____     Summary: _____

_____

Why do you think this movie will be popular?    _____

_____

2. Would these movies be popular in your home country? Why or why not? _____

_____

_____

_____

**PART II.        Go to the Internet and read the current status of the movies.**

What are the three most popular films right now?

1. _____  2. _____  3. _____

Did they match your predictions? Why or why not? What makes these films so popular?

_____

_____

# Activity 5.6

## Further Activities:

1. Have students see one of the movies and determine if they agree with the critical reviews of the film.

2. Have students work in pairs or small groups and write a review of a movie they saw.

3. Have students play the roles of movie critics (interviewers) and movie directors/script writers (interviewees).

## Modify the Level:

1. Beginning students can search for basic information about a movie, such as producer, director, actors, year made, and so on.

2. Intermediate students can do this activity in a modified form by excluding the "whys" on the worksheet. Students may state instead which movie they would most like to see and the reasons for their choice.

# Assessment

# A Rationale & Guide for Assessment in English Language Instruction

**Michelle Macy**

If integrating language skills and attending to variety in teaching methodologies offer students a maximized potential for learning success, it is essential that the measures of learner assessment utilized be consistent with those approaches. So often assessment of student progress does not reflect multiple teaching approaches, diverse learning strategies, or even the full range of the content covered. Language acquisition is an individualized experience dependent on many factors, including prior knowledge, motivation, socialization, teaching and learning styles, and so on. A movement away from standardized reading/writing tests toward a more integrated, comprehensive, and personalized system of evaluation is vital to providing the best possible language learning situation.

Traditional assessment has involved noncommunicative measures examining students' technical knowledge of a language, such as discrete grammar and vocabulary points, and using the degree of success on the test as a measure of overall level of mastery. These tests tended to be *norm referenced*, that is, they compared one student's performance to that of another, usually in a percentage scale format (e.g., 85 out of 100%). In addition, assessment was *summative* in nature, whereby a certain quantity of material was covered by the instructor, culminating in a single, comprehensive exam. Discrete-point tests play a role in assessment, since they help the instructor diagnose where specific material may or may not have entered into a student's language production. Tests such as these, however, offer an extremely incomplete and biased view of a learner's language proficiency. They completely fail to measure a student's ability to simultaneously make use of multiple skills to accomplish a communication task. They leave no means to account for developmental errors, which are so natural and unavoidable in language acquisition. What's more, tests such as these simply cannot measure a student's strategic or pragmatic competencies, nor do they consider a student's willingness to take risks and try new linguistic forms—to test hypotheses of language and to gain exposure to new linguistic information. Finally, such tests do not consider the notion that production (observed performance) may not reflect a student's competence (unobserved performance) due to a natural delay between the two.

In more recent years, greater emphasis has been placed on students' overall ability to communicate in the target language in a realistic and meaningful manner more consistent with a nonevaluative atmosphere. There has also been a switch to *criterion-referenced* assessments, which examine one's individual performance in terms of the degree to which one has met certain objectives (such as the current trend toward standards-based teaching). There is a movement away from summative evaluation toward *formative* assessment. The formative approach embeds assessment throughout learning in multiple forms, such as activities, games, peer reviews, and so on. The instructor is able to gain a much clearer perspective on students' emergent proficiency, as well as their progress over time.

Consistent with the integrative focus of this text teachers are encouraged to make formal oral and written evaluation subordinate to more holistic and revealing supporting data, such as that revealed in student portfolios and performance rubrics. Portfolios allow the teacher to see individual progress, which is important to establishing a definition of a student's "personal best," and for distinguishing between developmental errors (normal progress) and mistakes (which may need special attention). What's more, students can also see and measure their progress in the target language, which allows them to be more aware of and responsible for their own learning experiences. Performance rubrics allow for holistic, nondiscrete skill assessment of an individual's performance as part of the whole class and as a member of a group, as well as of informal and formal oral and written production. Presented in this chapter are four model performance rubrics, each devoted to a particular type of task, which you may wish to modify to a specific lesson.

Just as this book stresses integrating skills, it also stresses integrating evaluation techniques. Throughout the sample lessons you will find activities and worksheets that require a full range of communication skills and proficiencies. In addition to establishing emergent evaluation techniques with your students, such as portfolios of their work, you may also wish to consider employing the worksheets in conjunction with the rubrics in this chapter as assessment tools for individual and pair/group interactions, presentations, and compositions. The triangulation of observation obtained by assessing in multiple ways provides a much more accurate picture of an individual's proficiency in and progress toward appropriate and clear communication in the target language.

# INDIVIDUAL PRESENTATION RUBRIC

| | Self | | | Peer | | | Instructor | | |
|---|---|---|---|---|---|---|---|---|---|
| | EX | SA | NY | EX | SA | NY | EX | SA | NY |
| **Content** | | | | | | | | | |
| Relevance to class | | | | | | | | | |
| Interest to class | | | | | | | | | |
| Clarity of information | | | | | | | | | |
| Preparation | | | | | | | | | |
| Amount of information | | | | | | | | | |
| **Presentation** | | | | | | | | | |
| Organization | | | | | | | | | |
| Use of visuals | | | | | | | | | |
| Creativity | | | | | | | | | |
| Handouts | | | | | | | | | |
| **Communication** | | | | | | | | | |
| Effectiveness | | | | | | | | | |
| Natural speech (not read) | | | | | | | | | |
| Intonation/stress | | | | | | | | | |
| **Sources** | | | | | | | | | |
| Appropriateness | | | | | | | | | |
| Variety | | | | | | | | | |
| **Time** | | | | | | | | | |
| On time | | | | | | | | | |
| Respects presentation time allotted | | | | | | | | | |
| Pace, use of time | | | | | | | | | |
| **Overall effectiveness** | | | | | | | | | |

**Summary of Points**
Exemplary (EX) - 1 pt.
Satisfactory (SA) - 1/2 pt.
Not Yet (NY) - 0 pt.

**Total** _____ /18

# SMALL-GROUP PRESENTATION RUBRIC

| | Self | | | Peer | | | Instructor | | |
|---|---|---|---|---|---|---|---|---|---|
| | EX | SA | NY | EX | SA | NY | EX | SA | NY |
| **Content** | | | | | | | | | |
| Relevance to class | | | | | | | | | |
| Interest to class | | | | | | | | | |
| Clarity of information | | | | | | | | | |
| Preparation | | | | | | | | | |
| Amount of information | | | | | | | | | |
| **Presentation** | | | | | | | | | |
| Organization | | | | | | | | | |
| Use of visuals | | | | | | | | | |
| Creativity | | | | | | | | | |
| Handouts | | | | | | | | | |
| **Communication** | | | | | | | | | |
| Effectiveness | | | | | | | | | |
| Natural speech (not read) | | | | | | | | | |
| Intonation/stress | | | | | | | | | |
| **Sources** | | | | | | | | | |
| Appropriateness | | | | | | | | | |
| Variety | | | | | | | | | |
| **Time** | | | | | | | | | |
| On time | | | | | | | | | |
| Respects presentation time allotted | | | | | | | | | |
| Pace, use of time | | | | | | | | | |
| **Participation** | | | | | | | | | |
| All members | | | | | | | | | |
| **Overall Effectiveness** | | | | | | | | | |

**Summary of Points**
Exemplary (EX) - 1 pt.
Satisfactory (SA) - 1/2 pt.
Not Yet (NY) - 0 pt.

**Total** _____ /19

# PAIR/GROUP INTERACTION RUBRIC

| | Self | | | Peer | | | Instructor | | |
|---|---|---|---|---|---|---|---|---|---|
| | EX | SA | NY | EX | SA | NY | EX | SA | NY |
| **Interaction** | | | | | | | | | |
| Negotiation of meaning | | | | | | | | | |
| Interaction between/among participants | | | | | | | | | |
| **Communication** | | | | | | | | | |
| Effectiveness | | | | | | | | | |
| Level of language | | | | | | | | | |
| Use of language in context | | | | | | | | | |
| Natural speech (not read) | | | | | | | | | |
| Intonation/stress | | | | | | | | | |
| **Presentation** | | | | | | | | | |
| Organization | | | | | | | | | |
| Use of visuals/props | | | | | | | | | |
| Creativity | | | | | | | | | |
| Preparation | | | | | | | | | |
| Effort | | | | | | | | | |
| **Time** | | | | | | | | | |
| On time | | | | | | | | | |
| Respect presentation time allotted | | | | | | | | | |
| Pace, use of time | | | | | | | | | |
| **Overall effectiveness** | | | | | | | | | |

**Summary of Points**
Exemplary (EX) - 1 pt.
Satisfactory (SA) - 1/2 pt.
Not Yet (NY) - 0 pt.

**Total** _____ /16

# WRITING RUBRIC

| | Self | | | Peer | | | Instructor | | |
|---|---|---|---|---|---|---|---|---|---|
| | EX | SA | NY | EX | SA | NY | EX | SA | NY |
| **Introduction** | | | | | | | | | |
| Statement of the problem/issue | | | | | | | | | |
| Captures interest | | | | | | | | | |
| **Content** | | | | | | | | | |
| Relevance to lesson | | | | | | | | | |
| Clarity of information | | | | | | | | | |
| Preparation/effort | | | | | | | | | |
| Amount of information | | | | | | | | | |
| Organization | | | | | | | | | |
| Transitions | | | | | | | | | |
| Use of logic | | | | | | | | | |
| **Conclusion** | | | | | | | | | |
| Effectiveness | | | | | | | | | |
| Use of logic | | | | | | | | | |
| **Communication** | | | | | | | | | |
| Effectiveness | | | | | | | | | |
| Level of language | | | | | | | | | |
| Appropriateness to audience | | | | | | | | | |
| Spelling | | | | | | | | | |
| Syntax | | | | | | | | | |
| Vocabulary | | | | | | | | | |
| **Timeliness** | | | | | | | | | |
| First draft | | | | | | | | | |
| Final draft | | | | | | | | | |
| **Overall Effectiveness** | | | | | | | | | |

**Summary of Points**

Exemplary (EX) - 1 pt.

Satisfactory (SA) - 1/2 pt.

Not Yet (NY) - 0 pt.

Total _____ /20

# Tips for using Computers & the Internet

## Testing the Lesson

It is recommended that you connect to the Internet and attempt the lesson yourself, as if you were a student, prior to class. Remember that your students may need a bit more time than you do to complete the tasks involved.

## Adapting the Lesson

Should you wish to supplement or modify a lesson, additional sites can be easily located using keywords in a search engine.

*Note: a lesson and/or its accompanying worksheet may require slight modifications should you choose an alternative site.*

## Structuring the Lesson

Information offered on the Internet varies widely in quality and readability. Students may find difficulty looking for, accessing, and using information without structured directions from you prior to the lesson. A lack of clear, procedural instructions often results in student confusion and off-task behavior. It is advisable to review worksheet instructions, vocabulary, and content expectations, as well as directions for viewing Internet sites.

## Backup Lesson Plans

It is always wise to devise a backup lesson plan, since there is always the possibility of a technical failure when using computers and the Internet. Technical failures may occur in hardware students are to use, as well as that supporting Internet sites of interest. Always check that the necessary hardware and software are functioning on the computers your students will use, in addition to verifying the status of your computer lab's network, prior to the lesson.

## Limited Computer Access

If you have only a small number of computers available to your class, you may wish to have students complete different sections of the activity at different times.

## Dead and Modified Links

Due to the dynamic characteristics of the Internet, some sites may cease to exist or may acquire a new Internet address (URL). Prior to the lesson, verify that the provided sites are available. Should a site be unavailable, you may easily locate an alternative site using keywords in a search engine. On occasion, the site does not disappear, it just gets a new address. Try shortening the address/URL to relocate the site. (e.g., change http://goodhousekeeping.women.com/gh/advice/etiquette/00post21.htm to http://goodhousekeeping.women.com ).

*Note: a lesson and/or its accompanying worksheet may require slight modifications should you choose an alternative site.*

## Slow Connections

When working on the Internet, you may discover that the connection is slow. This may be due to several reasons:

- Traffic congestion at a specific website (too many visitors at one time)
- Traffic congestion in your own network (too many users of your Internet service are connected at the same time—especially with cable networks)
- Improper modem speed settings
- Computers with low processing or memory capacities

To avoid these situations, you may want to do the following:

- Avoid crowded sites by using alternative sites, or have students complete different sections of the activity at different times to minimize the number of users trying to gain access to a site at once.
- For those connecting to a server through a telephone line, you may wish to retry the connection, or to use alternative dial-up numbers for your Internet service.
- Avoid heavy traffic hours, such as before and after business lunch hours or closing time.
- Consult with your school's media specialist to optimize the connection.

## Student Computer Literacy

Students will come to the task with different levels of computer literacy and proficiency. You might want to assess their knowledge of computer use before engaging them in an activity. What's more, you may find computer literate students to be an invaluable resource in the classroom, both to you and to their peers.

## Firewalls

Firewalls provide greater Internet safety for your network by preventing people from accessing a system from the outside. Consult your school's media specialist concerning the requirements, installation, and settings for a firewall.

## Internet Safety

- Be certain that students know not to send or post any detailed personal information to noneducational (general) sites.

- Be also aware that some Internet sites contain material that is inappropriate for students to access. You may consider installing software (commercial or noncommercial freeware) that limits the type of sites your students may access.

- You may also want to establish an Internet "code of ethics" with your students, and develop a contract with them in terms of how they will use the Internet responsibly.

- Both you and your students need to be wary of e-mail from unknown or suspicious sources. Delete files that come from strangers or from companies from whom no information was requested, as they may contain virus files that can cause serious problems with computers and/or networks.

- As additional protection from viruses, be certain all computers are running the latest virus protection software. If this software does not have an automatic scanning function, ask students to scan any files they want to open or download from the Internet.

## Downloading

When downloading material from the Internet, be certain to comply with copyright laws. If you use any copyrighted material, you must conform to "fair use" restrictions. In many cases, material may be used for educational purposes, but may not be reproduced, broadcast or posted otherwise. For detailed information on fair use, visit related Internet sites, such as http://www.libraries.psu.edu/mtss/fairuse/default.html, or perform a search with "fair use" as keywords.

## Internet Searching

Many search engines provide tips for searching the Internet, and there exist websites devoted to searching tutorials, such as

- *How to search the WWW: A tutorial for beginners and nonexperts* at http://204.17.98.73/midlib/tutor.htm

- *Searching the web with* Yahoo! at http://howto.yahoo.com/chapters/7/1.html

- *Using* Alta Vista at http://www.aitech.ac.jp/~iteslj/th/1/ck-altavista.html.

Your own knowledge of and personal experience with searching the Internet may give you more confidence, and may enable you to help your students to understand more quickly and easily.

## Optimizing the Browser

Some of the Internet sites provided in this book cannot be viewed with an Internet browser alone. Additional functions or resources are occasionally necessary, such as JavaScript, Java applets, or any number of plug-ins. Ask your media specialist to set your browsers to enable those functions, or to install the required plug-ins (usually indicated in the lessons).

## Headphones or Headsets

For listening activities, personal headphones or headsets (headphones and microphone) may reduce interference.

## Recording Sound Files

When students are recording sound files, be certain that the microphone has been turned on, and that the sound recording software has been correctly configured. Verify also that the sound card and operating system have been set up properly.

## Additional Help

There are many listservs and discussion boards on distance learning, CALL (computer-assisted language learning), and instructional technology available to teachers encountering problems. Asking questions of your colleagues and of virtual learning experts may bring solutions to your problems, as well as fresh ideas for making use of the Internet in your classroom.

# GLOSSARY

**Adobe® Acrobat® Reader:** a program that allows users to view graphic and text files as the author intended them to appear.

**anglophone:** a speaker of English; referring to any culture where English is spoken.

**archive:** a library of computer files.

**audio/video clip:** sound/images that can be heard/shown on a computer.

**audio-/videoconferencing:** software programs that allow people to hear, see, and talk to each other on the Internet using headsets or speakers, microphones, and/or video cameras. Examples are NetMeeting® and Tribal Voice® Powwow®.

**brainstorm:** a collaborative process through which groups of people generate and refine ideas.

**browser:** a software application that enables the user to view websites on the Internet.

**CD-ROM (compact disc–read-only memory):** a disk that is inserted into a drive on the computer and which contains software or data.

**chat room:** Internet destinations where people can "talk" to each other by typing text back and forth; such conversations can involve pairs or groups.

**click:** to use the finger to press a mouse button once (click) to select, or twice (double-click) to open software or data files on a computer.

**cross-linguistic:** that which exists across languages; that which is common to a group of languages.

**debate:** a formally structured, arbitrated argument of a point or an issue, usually between two groups, and in which participants are given the opportunity to state opinions, support them, "rebut" (argue against) those of the opponent team, and in which a winner is often declared; governed by very strict rules.

**desktop:** the first screen to appear on most personal computers where the user can place and utilize frequently used file or application icons.

**download:** to bring software or data onto your computer's hard drive, usually from a website by use of a telephone line or network (wired or wireless) connection.

**downloading graphics:** with a PC, to place the cursor over the picture, click with the right button, and save in a file; with an Apple, to place the cursor over the picture, and hold down the mouse button for a few seconds until a menu comes up.

**e-card:** a message formatted as an electronic greeting card, sent via the Internet from one party to another.

**e-mail: (electronic mail):** sending and receiving messages through phone lines or networks using computer programs.

**emoticon:** the icon-like symbol often used in email messages where people use parentheses, colons, dashes and other symbols to depict "happy", "sad", "surprise" or other emotions (i.e., :-) , :-( , :-O , *^-^* , etc.).

**fair use:** guidelines governing the proper use of Internet materials without violating a party's rightful ownership of that material.

**firewall:** a means of blocking access to material on the Internet from unwanted or inappropriate parties.

**folder:** a graphic representation of an actual folder in which the user stores documents that belong together.

**hard drive:** a storage device on a computer.

**hardware:** the computer unit, viewing monitor, keyboard, and all other internal or external "object" parts of a computer system.

**homepage:** often the "beginning" or guide page of a URL (see *URL*), which provides access to other related sites on the Internet; also a personal website for an individual or other entity.

**HTML (Hypertext Markup Language):** programming language used to create Web pages.

**install:** the process of placing software on your hardware for ready accessibility.

**Internet:** a massive network or "web" of computers connected worldwide that allows users to share each other's information and programs; also called the "Net."

**key pal:** a pen pal reached through the Internet.

**keyword(s):** a word or words used when researching a topic on a browser that attempts to capture the "key" or central idea of the topic (example: *arthritis* might be a good keyword to use if one were searching for general information about joint ailments).

**links:** identifiable spots on a Web page that, when selected, take users to other referenced Web pages.

**load:** bringing new information in from another site on the Internet (or from software); usually involves some delay before the user can access the information fully.

**Local Area Network (LAN):** a network connecting a group of users "locally", that is, users in a study lab, school, part of an institution, or the like; LANs may be networked as well to enhance the capacity for users to chat, exchange files, or otherwise collaborate.

**login:** the procedure by which networks allow or deny a user to enter the system and use its resources.

**login name:** name chosen by the user (also called "username") to identify herself to the network.

**logoff:** to exit a network onto which one has previously logged on.

**logon:** see *login.*

**media player:** software designed for use with the Internet, which allows you to see or hear audio/video files.

**menu bar:** on both Windows and Mac OS operating systems, a design across the top of an open program window that offers a number of pull-down menus such as "File," "Format," "Edit," "Insert," and other common functions.

**Microsoft® Internet Explorer:** a Microsoft® corporation Internet browser somewhat similar to Netscape® Navigator with which users can view websites. Like Netscape®, Internet Explorer is a powerful tool for reading a variety of computer languages or scripts.

**Microsoft® Notepad for Windows®:** a simple text editor for the Windows® platform.

**Microsoft® Word:** a word processing program created and sold by the Microsoft® corporation.

**modem:** computer hardware that makes it possible for a computer to send and receive information via telephone lines.

**modem speed:** the amount of data a modem (computer network connection device using telephone lines) is able to pass through its wiring per second (i.e., 28.8 kilobytes per second) and the resulting speed of transfer of information.

**negotiation of meaning:** an interaction between speakers to resolve gaps in meaning.

**NetMeeting®:** see *audio-/videoconferencing*.

**Netscape® Navigator:** see *browser*, also see *Microsoft® Internet Explorer*.

**network:** the connecting of a number of computers by various means (telephone lines, radio waves, etc.) and with a variety of "protocols" or conventions.

**online:** connected to the Internet.

**onomatopoeic:** when the orthographic representation of a sound resembles the actual sound, for example, a cow's sound represented as *moo-oo* in English.

**operating system:** the main program controlling all the functions of a computer.

**plug-in:** software enhancements enabling the user's system to read a variety of audio and video files in a browser.

**portable document format (PDF) file:** a file created in the Adobe® Acrobat® proprietary file format.

**portfolio:** a collection over time (as opposed to a "snapshot") of student work that reflects a student's progress through what he has produced.

**presentation software:** application that enables users to create multimedia "slide shows" on the computer as an expedient, attractive way of presenting materials to others, such as Microsoft® PowerPoint®.

**program:** a set of codes with which one builds software.

**Real**™ **Audio**®/**Video**®/**Player**®: products created by RealNetworks™, which convey audio and video data.

**reload/refresh:** a means of updating data on a Web page.

**rubric:** an assessment instrument.

**schema building:** providing students with background information so they will be able to assimilate new material.

**scroll down:** to use arrows situated at the bottom or right side of the frame to view additional portions of the screen.

**search engine:** an Internet site dedicated to assisting people in their search for information on the Internet, which usually provides a simple format for typing in key words or clicking on topic areas to effectively locate the needed information.

**(search) field:** a space or area where a person may type in the key words or phrases for an Internet search.

**settings:** background configuration of a computer; selections made in various operating system programs that determine the functions the system will or will not perform.

**soap operas:** daytime television dramas popular in many cultures known for their exaggerated plots and melodramatic features.

**software:** a computer program that may accomplish any number of tasks from word processing to manipulating graphics.

**sound card:** a device that controls the input and output of sound on a computer.

**sound file:** a recording of sound in digital format.

**sound recording software:** a program that digitally encodes sound.

**StuffIt Expander**™: a program for Mac OS used to restore files that have been compressed (*see Win Zip*®).

**subplot:** a secondary story line.

**target culture:** the culture of the people speaking the target language (see *target language*).

**target language:** the language being studied by a group or individual.

**template:** a preformatted document intended to be used as a model.

**TexEdit Plus:** a simple text editor for the Mac OSX computer platform.

**text editors:** programs with which users can compose and manipulate text.

**toggle:** to go back and forth between applications or windows.

**travelogue:** a journal made while travelling, usually accompanied by photos.

**Tribal Voice® Powwow®:** see *audio-/videoconferencing.*

**URL (uniform resource locator):** an Internet address, most often designated by beginning *http:// .*

**VCR (videocassette recorder):** a video playback and recording machine.

**Web:** the array of computers and computer systems that can read HTML (see *HTML*) allowing users to navigate to a variety of connected sites on the Internet. (Also known as the *World Wide Web*).

**website:** a location on the Internet where information is posted.

**website addresses:** see *URL.*

**Win Zip®:** a program for PCs used to reduce or restore the size of a file in order to facilitate its transfer and use (see *StuffIt Expander™*).

**word processing program:** a software program used for typing and editing text.

**zip:** to reduce the size of a file to facilitate its transfer.

# INDEX

# ABOUT THE AUTHORS

**Carine M. Feyten** holds bachelor's and master's degrees in Germanic philology from the University of Louvain, Belgium, her home country. She is fluent in five languages and received her Ph.D. in interdisciplinary education. She is chair of the Department of Secondary Education at the University of South Florida, directs the Foreign Language Teacher Preparation Program, and codirects a Ph.D. program in second-language acquisition and instructional technology. She directs the Suncoast Alliance of Florida in Foreign Language and Literatures, was president of the Florida Foreign Language Association, and is currently second vice president of the National Network on Early Language Learning. She has won several teaching awards and one research award, has presented nationally and internationally, and has published in such journals as the *Modern Language Journal*, *The Middle School Journal* and *Language Quarterly*.

Dr. Carine M. Feyten

Chair, Secondary Education

University of South Florida

4202 East Fowler Avenue

Tampa, FL 33620 USA

feyten@tempest.coedu.usf.edu

**Michelle D. Macy** holds bachelor's and master's degrees in French language and literature. She is currently a visiting faculty member in the Department of Secondary Education at the University of South Florida, where she conducts courses associated with the Florida ESOL infusion program for preservice teachers, as well as internship supervision. She is presently completing a Ph.D. in second-language acquisition and instructional technology. She has taught both on-campus and overseas courses in French language and culture/civilization, and ESL/EFL. Her interests lie in SLA/instructional technology, ESOL, and teacher preparation.

Michelle D. Macy

Secondary Education

University of South Florida

4202 East Fowler Avenue; EDU 162

Tampa, FL 33620 USA

mmacy@tempest.coedu.usf.edu

**Jeannie Ducher** completed her *D.E.U.G.* and *Maîtrise* degrees in France in English language and civilization, and English literary translation, respectively. She is currently completing a Ph.D. in second-language acquisition and instructional technology at the University of South Florida. She has taught French language courses for the Division of Languages and Linguistics and currently teaches education courses for secondary education. She has also supervised preservice teachers during their field experiences. Her interests are in teacher education, SLA and technology and assessment using computer adaptive testing.

Jeannie Ducher

Secondary Education

University of South Florida

4202 East Fowler Avenue

Tampa, FL 33620 USA

jducher@tempest.coedu.usf.edu

**Makoto Yoshii** recently received his Ph.D. in second-language acquisition and instructional technology at the University of South Florida in Tampa, Florida. He holds a bachelor's degree in English literature from Kagoshima University in Japan, masters degrees in religious education and in divinity from Cincinnati Bible Seminary in Ohio, and a master's degree in applied linguistics from Indiana University. He is currently teaching EFL at Baiko Jo Gakuin College in Shimonoseki, Japan. He has taught both Japanese and ESL in the United States. His interests lie in CALL (computer-assisted language learning), particularly in the use of glosses in multimedia reading programs.

Makoto Yoshii

c/o English Language Institute

University of South Florida

4202 East Fowler Avenue; CPR 107

Tampa, FL 33620 USA

myoshii@luna.cas.usf.edu

**Eunwook Park** is pursuing a Ph.D. in second-language acquisition and instructional technology at the University of South Florida. He holds a bachelor's in French language and literature, with a minor in education, and a master's in French linguistics. He is a certified teacher of French in Korea, and has worked for various government organizations, as well as in the field of international business as a translator /interpreter. He has been working as a teaching assistant for the Florida ESOL infusion program for preservice teachers, using various recent technologies, such as video conferencing and Internet courseware. He is interested in wide range of CALL subjects, especially in teaching languages using the Internet for classroom or distance learning.

Eunwook Park

Secondary Education

University of South Florida, EDU 162

4202 E. Fowler Ave.

Tampa, FL 33620, USA

epark@tempest.coedu.usf.edu

**Brendan Calandra** is a Ph.D. student in instructional technology with a cognate in second-language acquisition at the University of South Florida. He has a masters degree from the University of Florida in German literature. Brendan currently works as a consultant for the Florida Center for Instructional Technology and teaches German for the Division of Languages and Linguistics at USF. He has been teaching modern languages at home and abroad since 1992.

Brendan Calandra

Florida Center for Instructional Technology

University of South Florida

4202 East Fowler Avenue

Tampa, FL 33620 USA

bcalandr@luna.cas.usf.edu

**John Meros** is a foreign language curriculum writer for the Melrose Center for Communications and Mass Media and a doctoral student at the University of South Florida in second-language acquisition and instructional technology. He has taught foreign language and ESOL for more than 17 years at various levels, cocreated the Pinellas district's acclaimed FLES (Elementary Foreign Language) program, and is now helping create the Melrose curriculum as he enters the Ph.D. candidate phase of his studies.

John Meros

Division of Languages and Linguistics

University of South Florida

4202 East Fowler Avenue; CPR 107

Tampa, FL 33620 USA

meros@chuma1.cas.usf.edu